The Loyal Subject by John Fletcher

John Fletcher was born in December, 1579 in Rye, Sussex. He was baptised on December 20th.

As can be imagined details of much of his life and career have not survived and, accordingly, only a very brief indication of his life and works can be given.

Young Fletcher appears at the very young age of eleven to have entered Corpus Christi College at Cambridge University in 1591. There are no records that he ever took a degree but there is some small evidence that he was being prepared for a career in the church.

However what is clear is that this was soon abandoned as he joined the stream of people who would leave University and decamp to the more bohemian life of commercial theatre in London.

The upbringing of the now teenage Fletcher and his seven siblings now passed to his paternal uncle, the poet and minor official Giles Fletcher. Giles, who had the patronage of the Earl of Essex may have been a liability rather than an advantage to the young Fletcher. With Essex involved in the failed rebellion against Elizabeth Giles was also tainted.

By 1606 John Fletcher appears to have equipped himself with the talents to become a playwright. Initially this appears to have been for the Children of the Queen's Revels, then performing at the Blackfriars Theatre.

Fletcher's early career was marked by one significant failure; The Faithful Shepherdess, his adaptation of Giovanni Battista Guarini's Il Pastor Fido, which was performed by the Blackfriars Children in 1608.

By 1609, however, he had found his stride. With his collaborator John Beaumont, he wrote Philaster, which became a hit for the King's Men and began a profitable association between Fletcher and that company. Philaster appears also to have begun a trend for tragicomedy.

By the middle of the 1610s, Fletcher's plays had achieved a popularity that rivalled Shakespeare's and cemented the pre-eminence of the King's Men in Jacobean London. After his frequent early collaborator John Beaumont's early death in 1616, Fletcher continued working, both singly and in collaboration, until his own death in 1625. By that time, he had produced, or had been credited with, close to fifty plays.

Index of Contents
DRAMATIS PERSONAE
THE SCENE: Mosco
PROLOGUE
ACTUS PRIMUS
SCÆNA PRIMA
SCÆNA SECUNDA
SCÆNA TERTIA
SCÆNA QUARTA
ACTUS SECUNDUS

SCÆNA PRIMA
SCÆNA SECUNDA
SCÆNA TERTIA
SCÆNA QUARTA
SCÆNA QUINTA
ACTUS TERTIUS
SCÆNA PRIMA
SCÆNA SECUNDA
SCÆNA TERTIA
SCÆNA QUARTA
SCÆNA QUINTA
SCÆNA SEXTA
ACTUS QUARTUS
SCÆNA PRIMA
SCÆNA SECUNDA
SCÆNA TERTIA
SCÆNA QUARTA
SCÆNA QUINTA
SCÆNA SEXTA
ACTUS QUINTUS
SCÆNA PRIMA
SCÆNA SECUNDA
SCÆNA TERTIA
SCÆNA QUARTA
SCÆNA QUINTA
SCÆNA SEXTA
EPILOGUE
JOHN FLETCHER – A SHORT BIOGRAPHY
JOHN FLETCHER – A CONCISE BIBLIOGRAPHY

DRAMATIS PERSONAE
MEN
Great Duke of Moscovia.
Archas, the Loyal Subject, General of the Moscovites.
Theodore, Son to Archas; valorous, but impatient.
Putskie alias Briskie, a Captain, Brother to Archas.
Alinda alias Archas, Son to Archas.
Burris, an honest Lord, the Dukes Favourite.
Boroskie, a malicious seducing Councellor to the Duke.
Ensign to Archas, a stout merry Souldier.
Souldiers.
Gentlemen.
Guard.
Servants.
Messengers, or Posts.
WOMEN

Olympia, Sister to the Duke.
Honora } Daughters of Archas.
Viola   }
Potesca } Servants to Olympia.
Ladies }
Bawd, a Court Lady.

THE SCENE: Mosco.

PROLOGUE

We need not noble Gentlemen to invite
Attention, preinstruct you who did write
This worthy Story, being confident
The mirth join'd with grave matter, and Intent
To yield the hearers profit, with delight,
Will speak the maker: and to do him right,
Would ask a Genius like to his; the age
Mourning his loss, and our now widdowed stage
In vain lamenting. I could adde, so far
Behind him the most modern writers are,
That when they would commend him, their best praise
Ruins the buildings which they strive to raise
To his best memory, so much a friend
Presumes to write, secure 'twill not offend
The living that are modest, with the rest
That may repine he cares not to contest.
This debt to Fletcher paid; it is profest
By us the Actors, we will do our best
To send such favouring friends, as hither come
To grace the Scene, pleas'd, and contented home.

ACTUS PRIMUS

SCÆNA PRIMA

Enter **THEODORE** and **PUTSKIE**.

THEODORE
Captain, your friend's prefer'd, the Princess has her,
Who, I assure my self, will use her nobly;
A pretty sweet one 'tis indeed.

PUTSKIE
Well bred, Sir,
I do deliver that upon my credit,
And of an honest stock.

THEODORE
It seems so, Captain,
And no doubt will do well.

PUTSKIE
Thanks to your care, Sir;
But tell me Noble Colonel, why this habit
Of discontent is put on through the Army?
And why your valiant Father, our great General,
The hand that taught to strike, the Love that led all;
Why he, that was the Father of the War,
He that begot, and bred the Souldier,
Why he sits shaking of his Arms, like Autumn,
His Colours folded, and his Drums cas'd up,
The tongue of War for ever ty'd within us?

THEODORE
It must be so: Captain you are a stranger,
But of a small time here a Souldier,
Yet that time shews ye a right good, and great one,
Else I could tell ye hours are strangely alter'd:
The young Duke has too many eyes upon him,
Too many fears 'tis thought too, and to nourish those,
Maintains too many Instruments.

PUTSKIE
Turn their hearts,
Or turn their heels up, Heaven: 'Tis strange it should be:
The old Duke lov'd him dearly.

THEODORE
He deserv'd it;
And were he not my Father, I durst tell ye,
The memorable hazards he has run through
Deserv'd of this man too; highly deserv'd too;
Had they been less, they had been safe Putskie,
And sooner reach'd regard.

PUTSKIE
There you struck sure, Sir.

THEODORE

Did I never tell thee of a vow he made
Some years before the old Duke dyed?

PUTSKIE
I have heard ye
Speak often of that vow; but how it was,
Or to what end, I never understood yet.

THEODORE
I'le tell thee then: and then thou wilt find the reason:
The last great Muster, ('twas before ye serv'd here,
Before the last Dukes death, whose honour'd bones
Now rest in peace) this young Prince had the ordering,
(To Crown his Fathers hopes) of all the Army:
Who (to be short) put all his power to practise;
Fashion'd, and drew 'em up: but alas, so poorly,
So raggedly and loosely, so unsouldier'd,
The good Duke blush'd, and call'd unto my Father,
Who then was General: Go, Archas, speedily,
And chide the Boy, before the Souldiers find him,
Stand thou between his ignorance and them,
Fashion their bodies new to thy direction;
Then draw thou up, and shew the Prince his errours.
My Sire obey'd, and did so; with all duty
Inform'd the Prince, and read him all directions:
This bred distaste, distaste grew up to anger,
And anger into wild words broke out thus:
Well, Archas, if I live but to command here,
To be but Duke once, I shall then remember.
I shall remember truly, trust me, I shall,
And by my Fathers hand—the rest his eyes spoke.
To which my Father answer'd (somewhat mov'd too)
And with a vow he seal'd it: Royal Sir,
Since for my faith and fights, your scorn and anger
Only pursue me; if I live to that day,
That day so long expected to reward me,
By his so ever noble hand you swore by,
And by the hand of Justice, never Arms more
Shall rib this body in, nor sword hang here, Sir:
The Conflicts I will do you service then in,
Shall be repentant prayers: So they parted.
The time is come; and now ye know the wonder.

PUTSKIE
I find a fear too, which begins to tell me,
The Duke will have but poor and slight defences,
If his hot humour raign, and not his honour:
How stand you with him, Sir?

THEODORE
A perdue Captain,
Full of my Fathers danger.

PUTSKIE
He has rais'd a young man,
They say a slight young man, I know him not,
For what desert?

THEODORE
Believe it, a brave Gentleman,
Worth the Dukes respect, a clear sweet Gentleman,
And of a noble soul: Come let's retire us,
And wait upon my Father, who within this hour
You will find an alter'd man.

PUTSKIE
I am sorry for't, Sir.

[Exeunt.

SCÆNA SECUNDA

Enter **OLYMPIA**, **PETESCA** and **GENTLEWOMAN**.

OLYMPIA
Is't not a handsome Wench?

GENTLEWOMAN
She is well enough, Madam:
I have seen a better face, and a straighter body,
And yet she is a pretty Gentlewoman.

OLYMPIA
What thinkst thou Petesca?

PETESCA
Alas, Madam, I have no skill, she has a black eye,
Which is of the least too, and the dullest water:
And when her mouth was made, for certain Madam,
Nature intended her a right good stomach.

OLYMPIA
She has a good hand.

GENTLEWOMAN
'Tis good enough to hold fast,
And strong enough to strangle the neck of a Lute.

OLYMPIA
What think ye of her colour?

PETESCA
If it be her own
'Tis good black blood: right weather-proof
I warrant it.

GENTLEWOMAN
What a strange pace she has got!

OLYMPIA
That's but her breeding.

PETESCA
And what a manly body! me thinks she looks
As though she would pitch the Bar, or go to Buffets.

GENTLEWOMAN
Yet her behaviour's utterly against it,
For me thinks she is too bashful.

OLYMPIA
Is that hurtful?

GENTLEWOMAN
Even equal to too bold: either of 'em, Madam,
May do her injury when time shall serve her.

OLYMPIA
You discourse learnedly, call in the wench.

[Exit **GENTLEWOMAN**

What envious fools are you? Is the rule general,
That Women can speak handsomly of none,
But those they are bred withal?

PETESCA
Scarce well of those, Madam,
If they believe they may out-shine 'em any way:
Our natures are like Oyl, compound us with any thing,
Yet still we strive to swim o' th' top:
Suppose there were here now,

Now in this Court of Mosco, a stranger Princess,
Of bloud and beauty equal to your excellence,
As many eyes and services stuck on her;
What would you think?

OLYMPIA
I would think she might deserve it.

PETESCA
Your Grace shall give me leave not to believe ye;
I know you are a Woman, and so humour'd:
I'le tell ye Madam, I could then get more Gowns on ye,
More Caps and Feathers, more Scarfs, and more Silk-stockings
With rocking you asleep with nightly railings
Upon that Woman, than if I had nine lives
I could wear out: by this hand ye'would scratch her eyes out.

OLYMPIA
Thou art deceiv'd fool;
Now let your own eye mock ye.

[Enter **GENTLEWOMAN** and **ALINDA**.

Come hither Girl: hang me and she be not a handsom one.

PETESCA
I fear it will prove indeed so.

OLYMPIA
Did you ever serve yet
In any place of worth?

ALINDA
No, Royal Lady.

PETESCA
Hold up your head; fie.

OLYMPIA
Let her alone, stand from her.

ALINDA
It shall be now,
Of all the blessings my poor youth has pray'd for,
The greatest and the happiest to serve you;
And might my promise carry but that credit
To be believ'd, because I am yet a stranger,
Excellent Lady, when I fall from duty,

From all the service that my life can lend me,
May everlasting misery then find me.

OLYMPIA
What think ye now? I do believe, and thank ye;
And sure I shall not be so far forgetful,
To see that honest faith die unrewarded:
What must I call your name?

ALINDA
Alinda, Madam.

OLYMPIA
Can ye sing?

ALINDA
A little, when my grief will give me leave, Lady.

OLYMPIA
What grief canst thou have Wench?
Thou art not in love?

ALINDA
If I be Madam, 'tis only with your goodness;
For yet I never saw that man I sighed for.

OLYMPIA
Of what years are you?

ALINDA
My Mother oft has told me,
That very day and hour this land was blest
With your most happy birth, I first saluted
This worlds fair light: Nature was then so busie,
And all the Graces to adorn your goodness,
I stole into the world poor and neglected.

OLYMPIA
Something there was, when I first look'd upon thee,
Made me both like and love thee: now I know it;
And you shall find that knowledge shall not hurt you:
I hope ye are a Maid?

ALINDA
I hope so too, Madam;
I am sure for any man: and were I otherwise,
Of all the services my hopes could point at,
I durst not touch at yours.

[Flourish. Enter **DUKE**, **BURRIS** and **GENTLEMAN**.

PETESCA
The great Duke, Madam.

DUKE
Good morrow, Sister.

OLYMPIA
A good day to your highness.

DUKE
I am come to pray you use no more perswasions
For this old stubborn man: nay to command ye:
His sail is swell'd too full: he is grown too insolent,
Too self-affected, proud: those poor slight services
He has done my Father, and my self, has blown him
To such a pitch, he flyes to stoop our favours.

OLYMPIA
I am sorry Sir: I ever thought those services
Both great and noble.

BURRIS
However, may it please ye
But to consider 'em a true hearts Servants,
Done out of faith to you, and not self-fame:
Do but consider royal Sir, the dangers;
When you have slept secure, the mid-night tempests,
That as he marcht sung through his aged locks;
When you have fed at full, the wants and famins;
The fires of Heaven, when you have found all temperate,
Death with his thousand doors—

DUKE
I have consider'd;
No more: and that I will have, shall be.

OLYMPIA
For the best,
I hope all still.

DUKE
What handsom wench is that there?

OLYMPIA
My Servant, Sir.

DUKE
Prethee observe her Burris,
Is she not wondrous handsom? speak thy freedom.

BURRIS
She appears no less to me Sir.

DUKE
Of whence is she?

OLYMPIA
Her Father I am told is a good Gentleman,
But far off dwelling: her desire to serve me
Brought her to th' Court, and here her friends have left her.

DUKE
She may find better friends:
Ye are welcom fair one,
I have not seen a sweeter: By your Ladies leave:
Nay stand up sweet, we'll have no superstition:
You have got a Servant; you may use him kindly,
And he may honour ye:

[Exit **DUKE** and **BURRIS**.

Good morrow Sister.

OLYMPIA
Good morrow to your Grace. How the wench blushes!
How like an Angel now she looks!

1ST WOMAN
At first jump
Jump into the Dukes arms? we must look to you,
Indeed we must, the next jump we are journeymen.

PETESCA
I see the ruine of our hopes already,
Would she were at home again, milking her Fathers Cows.

1ST WOMAN
I fear she'l milk all the great Courtiers first.

OLYMPIA
This has not made ye proud?

ALINDA

No certain, Madam.

OLYMPIA
It was the Duke that kist ye.

ALINDA
'Twas your Brother,
And therefore nothing can be meant but honour.

OLYMPIA
But say he love ye?

ALINDA
That he may with safety:
A Princes love extends to all his subjects.

OLYMPIA
But say in more particular?

ALINDA
Pray fear not:
For vertues sake deliver me from doubts, Lady:
'Tis not the name of King, nor all his promises,
His glories, and his greatness stuck about me,
Can make me prove a Traitor to your service:
You are my Mistris, and my noble Master,
Your vertues my ambition, and your favour
The end of all my love, and all my fortune:
And when I fail in that faith—

OLYMPIA
I believe thee,
Come wipe your eyes; I do: take you example—

PETESCA
I would her eyes were out.

1ST WOMAN
If the wind stand in this door,
We shall have but cold custome: some trick or other,
And speedily.

PETESCA
Let me alone to think on't.

OLYMPIA
Come, be you near me still.

ALINDA
With all my duty.

[Exeunt.

SCÆNA TERTIA

Enter **ARCHAS, THEODORE, PUTSKIE, ANCIENT** and **SOULDIERS**, carrying his armour piece-meale, his Colours wound up, and his Drums in Cases.

THEODORE
This is the heaviest march we e're trod Captain.

PUTSKIE
This was not wont to be: these honour'd pieces
The fierie god of war himself would smile at,
Buckl'd upon that body, were not wont thus,
Like Reliques to be offer'd to long rust,
And heavy-ey'd oblivion brood upon 'em.

ARCHAS
There set 'em down: and glorious war farewel;
Thou child of honour and ambitious thoughts,
Begot in bloud, and nurs'd with Kingdomes ruines;
Thou golden danger, courted by thy followers
Through fires and famins, for one title from thee—
Prodigal man-kind spending all his fortunes;
A long farewel I give thee: Noble Arms,
You ribs for mighty minds, you Iron houses,
Made to defie the thunder-claps of Fortune,
Rust and consuming time must now dwell with ye:
And thou good Sword that knewst the way to conquest,
Upon whose fatal edge despair and death dwelt,
That when I shook thee thus, fore-shew'd destruction,
Sleep now from bloud, and grace my Monument:
Farewel my Eagle; when thou flew'st, whole Armies
Have stoopt below thee: At Passage I have seen thee,
Ruffle the Tartars, as they fled thy furie;
And bang 'em up together, as a Tassel,
Upon the streach, a flock of fearfull Pigeons.
I yet remember when the Volga curl'd,
The aged Volga, when he heav'd his head up,
And rais'd his waters high, to see the ruins;
The ruines our Swords made, the bloudy ruins,
Then flew this Bird of honour bravely, Gentlemen;
But these must be forgotten: so must these too,

And all that tend to Arms, by me for ever.
Take 'em you holy men; my Vow take with 'em,
Never to wear 'em more: Trophies I give 'em,
And sacred Rites of war to adorn the Temple:
There let 'em hang, to tell the world their master
Is now Devotions Souldier, fit for prayer.
Why do ye hang your heads? why look you sad friends?
I am not dying yet.

THEODORE
Ye are indeed to us Sir.

PUTSKIE
Dead to our fortunes, General.

ARCHAS
You'l find a better,
A greater, and a stronger man to lead ye,
And to a stronger fortune: I am old, friends,
Time, and the wars together make me stoop, Gentlemen,
Stoop to my grave: my mind unfurnish'd too,
Emptie and weak as I am: my poor body,
Able for nothing now but contemplation,
And that will be a task too to a Souldier:
Yet had they but encourag'd me, or thought well
Of what I have done, I think I should have ventur'd
For one knock more, I should have made a shift yet
To have broke one staff more handsomly, and have died
Like a good fellow, and an honest Souldier,
In the head of ye all, with my Sword in my hand,
And so have made an end of all with credit.

THEODORE
Well, there will come an hour, when all these injuries,
These secure slights—

ARCHAS
Ha! no more of that sirrah,
Not one word more of that I charge ye.

THEODORE
I must speak Sir.
And may that tongue forget to sound your service,
That's dumb to your abuses.

ARCHAS
Understand fool,
That voluntary I sit down.

THEODORE
You are forced, Sir,
Forced for your safety: I too well remember
The time and cause, and I may live to curse 'em:
You made this Vow, and whose unnobleness,
Indeed forgetfulness of good—

ARCHAS
No more,
As thou art mine no more.

THEODORE
Whose doubts and envies—
But the Devil will have his due.

PUTSKIE
Good gentle Colonel.

THEODORE
And though disgraces, and contempt of Honour
Reign now, the Wheel must turn again.

ARCHAS
Peace Sirrah,
Your tongue's too saucy: do you stare upon me?
Down with that heart, down suddenly, down with it,
Down with that disobedience; tye that tongue up.

THEODORE
Tongue?

ARCHAS
Do not provoke me to forget my Vow, Sirrah.
And draw that fatal Sword again in anger.

PUTSKIE
For Heavens sake, Colonel.

ARCHAS
Do not let me doubt
Whose Son thou art, because thou canst not suffer:
Do not play with mine anger; if thou dost,
By all the Loyalty my heart holds—

THEODORE
I have done, Sir,
Pray pardon me.

ARCHAS
I pray be worthy of it:
Beshrew your heart, you have vext me.

THEODORE
I am sorry, Sir.

ARCHAS
Go to, no more of this: be true and honest,
I know ye are man enough, mould it to just ends,
And let not my disgraces, then I am miserable,
When I have nothing left me but thy angers.

[Flourish. Enter **DUKE**, **BURRIS**, **BOROSKIE**, **ATTENDANTS** and **GENTLEMAN**.

PUTSKIE
And't please ye, Sir, the Duke.

DUKE
Now, what's all this?
The meaning of this ceremonious Emblem?

ARCHAS
Your Grace should first remember—

BOROSKIE
There's his Nature.

DUKE
I do, and shall remember still that injury,
That at the Muster, where it pleas'd your Greatness
To laugh at my poor Souldiership, to scorn it;
And more to make me seem ridiculous,
Took from my hands my charge.

BURRIS
O think not so, Sir.

DUKE
And in my Fathers sight.

ARCHAS
Heaven be my witness,
I did no more, (and that with modesty,
With Love and Faith to you) than was my warrant,
And from your Father seal'd: nor durst that rudeness,
And impudence of scorn fall from my 'haviour,

I ever yet knew duty.

DUKE
We shall teach ye,
I well remember too, upon some words I told ye,
Then at that time, some angry words ye answer'd,
If ever I were Duke, you were no Souldier.
You have kept your word, and so it shall be to you,
From henceforth I dismiss you; take your ease, Sir.

ARCHAS
I humbly thank your Grace; this wasted Body,
Beaten and bruis'd with Arms, dry'd up with troubles,
Is good for nothing else but quiet, now Sir,
And holy Prayers; in which, when I forget
To thank Heaven for all your bounteous favours,
May that be deaf, and my Petitions perish.

BOROSKIE
What a smooth humble Cloak he has cas'd his pride in!
And how he has pull'd his Claws in! there's no trusting—

BURRIS
Speak for the best.

BOROSKIE
Believe I shall do ever.

DUKE
To make ye understand, we feel not yet
Such dearth of Valour, and Experience,
Such a declining Age of doing Spirits,
That all should be confin'd within your excellence,
And you, or none be honour'd, take Boroskie,
The place he has commanded, lead the Souldier;
A little time will bring thee to his honour,
Which has been nothing but the Worlds opinion,
The Souldiers fondness, and a little fortune,
Which I believe his Sword had the least share in.

THEODORE
O that I durst but answer now.

PUTSKIE
Good Colonel.

THEODORE
My heart will break else: Royal Sir, I know not

What you esteem mens lives, whose hourly labours,
And loss of Blood, consumptions in your service,
Whose Bodies are acquainted with more miseries,
And all to keep you safe, than Dogs or Slaves are.
His Sword the least share gain'd?

DUKE
You will not fight with me?

THEODORE
No Sir, I dare not,
You are my Prince, but I dare speak to ye,
And dare speak truth, which none of their ambitions
That be informers to you, dare once think of;
Yet truth will now but anger ye; I am sorry for't,
And so I take my leave.

[Exit.

DUKE
Ev'n when you please, Sir.

ARCHAS
Sirrah, see me no more.

DUKE
And so may you too:
You have a house i'th' Country, keep you there, Sir,
And when you have rul'd your self, teach your Son manners,
For this time I forgive him.

ARCHAS
Heaven forgive all;
And to your Grace a happy and long Rule here.
And you Lord General, may your fights be prosperous.
In all your Course may Fame and Fortune court you.
Fight for your Country, and your Princes safety;
Boldly, and bravely face your Enemy,
And when you strike, strike with that killing Vertue,
As if a general Plague had seiz'd before ye;
Danger, and doubt, and labour cast behind ye;
And then come home an old and noble Story.

BURRIS
A little comfort, Sir.

DUKE
As little as may be:

Farewel, you know your limit.

[Exit **DUKE**, &c.

BURRIS
Alas, brave Gentleman.

ARCHAS
I do, and will observe it suddenly,
My Grave; I, that's my limit; 'tis no new thing,
Nor that can make me start, or tremble at it,
To buckle with that old grim Souldier now:
I have seen him in his sowrest shapes, and dreadfull'st;
I, and I thank my honesty, have stood him:
That audit's cast; farewel my honest Souldiers,
Give me your hands; farewel, farewel good Ancient,
A stout man, and a true, thou art come in sorrow.
Blessings upon your Swords, may they ne'r fail ye;
You do but change a man; your fortune's constant;
That by your ancient Valours is ty'd fast still;
Be valiant still, and good: and when ye fight next,
When flame and fury make but one face of horrour,
When the great rest of all your honour's up,
When you would think a Spell to shake the enemy,
Remember me, my Prayers shall be with ye:
So once again farewel.

PUTSKIE
Let's wait upon ye.

ARCHAS
No, no, it must not be; I have now left me
A single Fortune to my self, no more,
Which needs no train, nor complement; good Captain,
You are an honest and a sober Gentleman,
And one I think has lov'd me.

PUTSKIE
I am sure on't.

ARCHAS
Look to my Boy, he's grown too headstrong for me.
And if they think him fit to carry Arms still,
His life is theirs; I have a house i'th' Country,
And when your better hours will give you liberty,
See me: you shall be welcome. Fortune to ye.

[Exit.

ANCIENT
I'll cry no more, that will do him no good,
And 'twill but make me dry, and I have no money:
I'll fight no more, and that will do them harm;
And if I can do that, I care not for money:
I could have curst reasonable well, and I have had the luck too
To have 'em hit sometimes. Whosoever thou art,
That like a Devil didst possess the Duke
With these malicious thoughts; mark what I say to thee,
A Plague upon thee, that's but the Preamble.

SOULDIER
O take the Pox too.

ANCIENT
They'll cure one another;
I must have none but kills, and those kill stinking:
Or look ye, let the single Pox possess them,
Or Pox upon Pox.

PUTSKIE
That's but ill i'th' arms, Sir.

ANCIENT
'Tis worse i'th' Legs, I would not wish it else:
And may those grow to scabs as big as Mole-hills,
And twice a day, the Devil with a Curry-Comb
Scratch 'em, and scrub 'em: I warrant him he has 'em.

SOULDIER
May he be ever lowzie.

ANCIENT
That's a pleasure,
The Beggar's Lechery; sometimes the Souldiers:
May he be ever lazie, stink where he stands,
And Maggots breed in's Brains.

2ND SOULDIER
I, marry Sir,
May he fall mad in love with his Grand-mother,
And kissing her, may her teeth drop into his mouth,
And one fall cross his throat, then let him gargle.

[Enter a **POST**.

PUTSKIE

Now, what's the matter?

POST
Where's the Duke, pray, Gentlemen?

PUTSKIE
Keep on your way, you cannot miss.

POST
I thank ye.

[Exit.

ANCIENT
If he be married, may he dream he's cuckol'd,
And when he wakes believe, and swear he saw it,
Sue a Divorce, and after find her honest:
Then in a pleasant Pigstye, with his own garters,
And a fine running knot, ride to the Devil.

PUTSKIE
If these would do—

ANCIENT
I'll never trust my mind more,
If all these fail.

1ˢᵀ SOULDIER
What shall we do now, Captain?
For by this honest hand I'll be torn in pieces,
Unless my old General go, or some that love him,
And love us equal too, before I fight more:
I can make a Shooe yet, and draw it on too,
If I like the Leg well.

ANCIENT
Fight? 'tis likely:
No, there will be the sport Boys, when there's need on's.
They think the other Crown will do, will carry us,
And the brave golden Coat of Captain Cankro
Boroskie. What a noise his very name carries!
'Tis Gun enough to fright a Nation,
He needs no Souldiers; if he do, for my part,
I promise ye he's like to seek 'em; so I think you think too,
And all the Army; No, honest, brave old Archas,
We cannot so soon leave thy memory,
So soon forget thy goodness: he that does,
The scandal and the scumm of Arms be counted.

PUTSKIE
You much rejoice me now you have hit my meaning,
I durst not press ye, till I found your spirits:
Continue thus.

ANCIENT
I'll go and tell the Duke on't.

[Enter **2ND POST**.

PUTSKIE
No, no, he'll find it soon enough, and fear it,
When once occasion comes: Another Packet!
From whence, Friend, come you?

2ND POST
From the Borders, Sir.

PUTSKIE
What news, Sir, I beseech you?

2ND POST
Fire and Sword, Gentlemen;
The Tartar's up, and with a mighty force,
Comes forward, like a tempest, all before him
Burning and killing.

ANCIENT
Brave Boys, brave news, Boys.

2ND POST
Either we must have present help—

ANCIENT
Still braver.

2ND POST
Where lies the Duke?

SOULDIER
He's there.

2ND POST
'Save ye, Gentlemen.

[Exit.

ANCIENT
We are safe enough, I warrant thee:
Now the time's come.

PUTSKIE
I, now 'tis come indeed, and now stand firm, Boys,
And let 'em burn on merrily.

ANCIENT
This City would make a fine marvellous Bone-fire:
'Tis old dry timber, and such Wood has no fellow.

2ND SOULDIER
Here will be trim piping anon and whining,
Like so many Pigs in a storm,
When they hear the news once.

[Enter **BOROSKIE** and **SERVANT**.

PUTSKIE
Here's one has heard it already;
Room for the General.

BOROSKIE
Say I am faln exceeding sick o'th' sudden,
And am not like to live.

PUTSKIE
If ye go on, Sir,
For they will kill ye certainly; they look for ye.

ANCIENT
I see your Lordship's bound, take a suppository,
'Tis I, Sir; a poor cast Flag of yours. The foolish Tartars
They burn and kill, and't like your honour, kill us,
Kill with Guns, with Guns my Lord, with Guns, Sir.
What says your Lordship to a chick in sorrel sops?

PUTSKIE
Go, go thy ways old true-penny;
Thou hast but one fault: thou art ev'n too valiant.
Come, to'th' Army Gentlemen, and let's make them acquainted.

SOULDIER
Away, we are for ye.

[Exeunt.

SCÆNA QUARTA

Enter **ALINDA**, **PETESCA** and **GENTLEWOMAN**.

ALINDA
Why, whither run ye Fools; will ye leave my Lady?

PETESCA
The Tartar comes, the Tartar comes.

ALINDA
Why, let him,
I thought you had fear'd no men: upon my conscience
You have try'd their strengths already; stay for shame.

PETESCA
Shift for thy self, Alinda.

[Exit.

ALINDA
Beauty bless ye:
Into what Grooms Feather-Bed will you creep now?
And there mistake the enemy; sweet youths ye are,
And of a constant courage; are you afraid of foining?

[Enter **OLYMPIA**.

OLYMPIA
O my good Wench, what shall become of us?
The Posts come hourly in, and bring new danger;
The enemy is past the Volga, and bears hither
With all the blood and cruelty he carries,
My Brother now will find his fault.

ALINDA
I doubt me,
Somewhat too late, Madam. But pray fear not,
All will be well, I hope. Sweet Madam, shake not.

OLYMPIA
How cam'st thou by this Spirit? our Sex trembles.

ALINDA
I am not unacquainted with these dangers;
And you shall know my truth; for ere you perish,

A hundred Swords shall pass through me: 'tis but dying,
And Madam we must do it: the manner's all:
You have a Princely Birth, take Princely thoughts to you,
And take my counsel too; go presently,
With all the haste ye have, (I will attend ye)
With all the possible speed, to old Lord Archas,
He honours ye; with all your art perswade him,
('Twill be a dismal time else) woo him hither,
But hither Madam, make him see the danger;
For your new General looks like an Ass;
There's nothing in his face but loss.

OLYMPIA
I'll do it.
And thank thee, sweet Alinda: O my Jewel,
How much I'm bound to love thee! by this hand, Wench,
If thou wert a man—

ALINDA
I would I were to fight for you.
But haste dear Madam.

OLYMPIA
I need no Spurs Alinda.

SCEANA QUINTA

Enter **DUKE, TWO POSTS, ATTENDANTS, GENTLEMEN.**

DUKE
The Lord General sick now? is this a time
For men to creep into their Beds? What's become, Post,
Of my Lieutenant?

POST
Beaten, and't please your Grace,
And all his Forces sparkled.

[Enter a **GENTLEMAN**.

DUKE
That's but cold news:
How now, what good news? are the Souldiers ready?

GENTLEMAN
Yes Sir, but fight they will not, nor stir from that place

They stand in now, unless they have Lord Archas
To lead 'em out; they rail upon this General,
And sing Songs of him, scurvy Songs, to worse tunes:
And much they spare not you, Sir: here they swear
They'll stand and see the City burnt, and dance about it,
Unless Lord Archas come before they fight for't:
It must be so, Sir.

DUKE
I could wish it so too;
And to that end I have sent Lord Burris to him;
But all I fear will fail; we must dye, Gentlemen,
And one stroke we'll have for't.

[Enter **BURRIS**.

What bring'st thou, Burris?

BURRIS
That I am loth to tell; he will not come, Sir;
I found him at his Prayers, there he tells me,
The Enemy shall take him, fit for Heaven:
I urg'd to him all our dangers, his own worths,
The Countries ruine; nay I kneel'd and pray'd him;
He shook his head, let fall a tear, and pointed
Thus with his finger to the Ground; a Grave
I think he meant; and this was all he answer'd.
Your Grace was much to blame:
Where's the new General?

DUKE
He is sick, poor man.

BURRIS
He's a poor man indeed, Sir:
Your Grace must needs go to the Souldier.

DUKE
They have sent me word
They will not stir, they rail at me,
And all the spight they have—

[Shout within.

What shout is that there?
Is the Enemy come so near?

[Enter **ARCHAS**, **OLYMPIA** and **ALINDA**.

OLYMPIA
I have brought him, Sir,
At length I have woo'd him thus far.

DUKE
Happy Sister,
O blessed Woman!

OLYMPIA
Use him nobly, Brother;
You never had more need: And Gentlemen,
All the best powers ye have, to tongues turn presently,
To winning and perswading tongues: all my art,
Only to bring him hither, I have utter'd;
Let it be yours to arm him; And good my Lord,
Though I exceed the limit you allow'd me,
Which was the happiness to bring ye hither,
And not to urge ye farther; yet, see your Country,
Out of your own sweet Spirit now behold it:
Turn round, and look upon the miseries,
On every side the fears; O see the dangers;
We find 'em soonest, therefore hear me first, Sir.

DUKE
Next hear your Prince:
You have said you lov'd him, Archas,
And thought your life too little for his service;
Think not your vow too great now, now the time is,
And now you are brought to th' test, touch right now Souldier,
Now shew the manly pureness of thy mettle;
Now if thou beest that valued man, that vertue,
That great obedience teaching all, now stand it.
What I have said forget, my youth was hasty,
And what you said your self forgive, you were angry.
If men could live without their faults, they were gods, Archas.
He weeps, and holds his hands up: to him, Burris.

BURRIS
You have shew'd the Prince his faults;
And like a good Surgeon you have laid
That to 'em makes 'em smart; he feels it,
Let 'em not fester now, Sir; your own honour,
The bounty of that mind, and your allegiance,
'Gainst which I take it, Heaven gives no Command, Sir,
Nor seals no Vow, can better teach ye now
What ye have to do, than I, or this necessity;
Only this little's left; would ye do nobly,

And in the Eye of Honour truly triumph?
Conquer that mind first, and then men are nothing.

ALINDA
Last, a poor Virgin kneels; for loves sake General,
If ever you have lov'd; for her sake, Sir,
For your own honesty, which is a Virgin,
Look up, and pity us, be bold and fortunate,
You are a Knight, a good and noble Souldier,
And when your Spurs were given ye, your Sword buckl'd,
Then were you sworn for Vertues Cause, for Beauties,
For Chastity to strike; strike now, they suffer;
Now draw your Sword, or else you are recreant,
Only a Knight i'th' Heels, i'th' Heart a Coward;
Your first Vow honour made, your last but anger.

ARCHAS
How like my vertuous Wife this thing looks, speaks too?
So would she chide my dulness: fair one, I thank ye.
My gracious Sir, your pardon, next your hand:
Madam, your favour, and your prayers: Gentlemen,
Your wishes, and your loves: and pretty sweet one,
A favour for your Souldier.

OLYMPIA
Give him this, Wench.

ALINDA
Thus do I tye on Victory.

ARCHAS
My Armour,
My Horse, my Sword, my tough Staff, and my Fortune,
And Olin now I come to shake thy glory.

DUKE
Go, brave and prosperous, our loves go with thee.

OLYMPIA
Full of thy vertue, and our Prayers attend thee.

BURRIS &c.
Loaden with Victory, and we to honour thee.

ALINDA
Come home the Son of Honour,
And I'll serve ye.

[Exeunt.

ACTUS SECUNDUS

SCÆNA PRIMA

Enter **DUKE**, **BURRIS**, and two **GENTLEMEN**.

DUKE
No news of Archas yet?

BURRIS
But now, and't please ye,
A Post came in, Letters he brought none with him,
But this deliver'd: He saw the Armies join,
The game of Blood begun, and by our General,
Who never was acquainted but with Conquest,
So bravely fought, he saw the Tartars shaken,
And there he said he left 'em.

DUKE
Where's Boroskie?

1ST GENTLEMAN
He's up again, and't please ye.

BURRIS
Sir, methinks
This News should make ye lightsome, bring joy to ye,
It strikes our hearts with general Comfort.

[Exit **DUKE**.

Gone? What should this mean, so suddenly?
He's well?

2ND GENTLEMAN
We see no other.

1ST GENTLEMAN
Would the rest were well too,
That put these starts into him.

BURRIS
I'll go after him.

2ND GENTLEMAN
'Twill not be fit, Sir: h'as some secret in him
He would not be disturb'd in: know you any thing
Has crost him since the General went?

BURRIS
Not any:
If there had been, I am sure I should have found it:
Only I have heard him oft complain for money:
Money he says he wants.

1ST GENTLEMAN
It may be that then.

BURRIS
To him that has so many wayes to raise it,
And those so honest, it cannot be.

[Enter **DUKE** and **BOROSKIE**.

1ST GENTLEMAN
He comes back,
And Lord Boroskie with him.

BURRIS
There the game goes,
I fear some new thing hatching.

DUKE
Come hither Burris.
Go see my Sister, and commend me to her,
And to my little Mistriss give this Token;
Tell her I'le see her shortly.

BURRIS
Yes, I shall, Sir.

[Exit **BURRIS** and **GENTLEMAN**.

DUKE
Wait you without: I would yet try him further.

BOROSKIE
'Twill not be much amiss: has your Grace heard yet
Of what he has done i'th' Field?

DUKE
A Post but now

Came in, who saw 'em joyn, and has delivered,
The Enemy gave ground before he parted.

BOROSKIE
'Tis well.

DUKE
Come, speak thy mind man: 'tis not for fighting,
A noise of War, I keep thee in my bosom;
Thy ends are nearer to me; from my Childhood
Thou brought'st me up: and like another nature,
Made good all my necessities: speak boldly.

BOROSKIE
Sir, what I utter, will be thought but envy
Though I intend, high heaven knows, but your honour,
When vain and empty people shall proclaim me—
Good Sir excuse me.

DUKE
Do you fear me for your Enemy?
Speak on your duty.

BOROSKIE
Then I must, and dare, Sir:
When he comes home, take heed the Court receive him not,
Take heed he meet not with their loves and praises,
That Glass will shew him ten times greater, Sir,
(And make him strive to make good that proportion,)
Than ere his fortune bred him, he is honourable,
At least I strive to understand him so,
And of a nature, if not this way poyson'd,
Perfect enough, easie, and sweet, but those are soon seduc'd, Sir;
He's a great man, and what that Pill may work,
Prepar'd by general voices of the people,
Is the end of all my Counsel, only this, Sir,
Let him retire a while, there's more hangs by it
Than you know yet: there if he stand a while well,
But till the Souldier cool, whom, for their service
You must pay now most liberally, most freely,
And showre your self into 'em; 'tis the bounty
They follow with their loves, and not the bravery.

[Enter **TWO GENTLEMAN**.

DUKE
But where's the Money? how now?

2ND GENTLEMAN
Sir, the Colonel,
Son to the Lord Archas, with most happy news
Of the Tartars overthrow, without here
Attends your Graces pleasure.

BOROSKIE
Be not seen, Sir,
He's a bold fellow, let me stand his Thunders,
To th' Court he must not come: no blessing here, Sir,
No face of favour, if you love your honour.

[Enter **THEODORE**.

DUKE
Do what you think is meetest; I'le retire, Sir.

[Exit.

BOROSKIE
Conduct him in, Sir—welcome noble Colonel.

THEODORE
That's much from your Lordship: pray where's the Duke?

BOROSKIE
We hear you have beat the Tartar.

THEODORE
Is he busie, Sir?

BOROSKIE
Have ye taken Olin yet?

THEODORE
I would fain speak with him.

BOROSKIE
How many men have ye lost?

THEODORE
Do's he lye this way?

BOROSKIE
I am sure you fought it bravely.

THEODORE
I must see him.

BOROSKIE
You cannot yet, ye must not, what's your Commission?

THEODORE
No Gentleman o'th' Chamber here?

BOROSKIE
Why, pray ye, Sir?
Am not I fit to entertain your business?

THEODORE
I think you are not, Sir; I am sure ye shall not.
I bring no tales, nor flatteries: in my tongue, Sir,
I carry no fork'd stings.

BOROSKIE
You keep your bluntness.

THEODORE
You are deceiv'd: it keeps me: I had felt else
Some of your plagues ere this: but good Sir trifle not,
I have business to the Duke.

BOROSKIE
He's not well, Sir,
And cannot now be spoke withal.

THEODORE
Not well, Sir?
How would he ha' been, if we had lost? not well, Sir?
I bring him news to make him well: his enemy
That would have burnt his City here, and your House too,
Your brave gilt house, my Lord, your honours hangings,
Where all your Ancestors, and all their Battels,
Their silk and golden Battels are decipher'd:
That would not only have abus'd your buildings,
Your goodly buildings, Sir, and have drunk dry your butteries,
Purloin'd your Lordships Plate, the Duke bestow'd on you,
For turning handsomly o'th' toe, and trim'd your Virgins,
Trim'd 'em of a new cut, and't like your Lordship,
'Tis ten to one, your Wife too, and the curse is
You had had no remedy against these Rascals,
No Law, and't like your Honour; would have kill'd you too
And roasted ye, and eaten ye, ere this time:
Notable Knaves my Lord, unruly Rascals:
These youths have we ty'd up, put muzzels on 'em,
And par'd their Nails, that honest civil Gentlemen,

And such most noble persons as your self is,
May live in peace, and rule the land with a twine thread.
These news I bring.

BOROSKIE
And were they thus deliver'd ye?

THEODORE
My Lord, I am no pen-man, nor no Orator,
My tongue was never Oyl'd with Here and't like ye,
There I beseech ye, weigh, I am a Souldier,
And truth I covet only, no fine terms, Sir;
I come not to stand treating here; my business
Is with the Duke, and of such general blessing—

BOROSKIE
You have overthrown the enemy, we know it,
And we rejoyce in't; ye have done like honest Subjects,
You have done handsomely and well.

THEODORE
But well, Sir?
But handsomely and well? what are we juglers?
I'le do all that in cutting up a Capon.
But handsomely and well? does your Lordship take us
For the Dukes Tumblers? we have done bravely, Sir,
Ventur'd our lives like men.

BOROSKIE
Then bravely be it.

THEODORE
And for as brave rewards we look, and graces,
We have sweat and bled for't, Sir.

BOROSKIE
And ye may have it,
If you will stay the giving. Men that thank themselves first
For any good they do, take off the lustre,
And blot the benefit.

THEODORE
Are these the welcomes,
The Bells that ring out our rewards? pray heartily,
Early and late, there may be no more Enemies:
Do my good Lord, pray seriously, and sigh too,
For if there be—

BOROSKIE
They must be met, and fought with.

THEODORE
By whom? by you? they must be met and flatter'd.
Why, what a Devil ail'd ye to do these things?
With what assurance dare ye mock men thus?
You have but single lives, and those I take it
A Sword may find too: why do ye dam the Duke up?
And choak that course of love, that like a River
Should fill our empty veins again with comforts?
But if ye use these knick knacks,
This fast and loose, with faithful men and honest,
You'l be the first will find it.

[Enter **ARCHAS, SOULDIERS, PUTSKIE, ANCIENT** and **OTHERS**.

BOROSKIE
You are too untemperate.

THEODORE
Better be so, and thief too, than unthankful:
Pray use this old man so, and then we are paid all.
The Duke thanks ye for your service, and the Court thanks ye,
And wonderful desirous they are to see ye;
Pray Heaven we have room enough to march for May-games,
Pageants, and Bone-fires for your welcome home, Sir.
Here your most noble friend the Lord Boroskie,
A Gentleman too tender of your credit,
And ever in the Dukes ear, for your good, Sir,
Crazie and sickly, yet to be your servant,
Has leapt into the open air to meet ye.

BOROSKIE
The best is, your words wound not, you are welcome home, Sir;
Heartily welcome home, and for your service,
The noble overthrow you gave the Enemy,
The Duke salutes ye too with all his thanks, Sir.

ANCIENT
Sure they will now regard us.

PUTSKIE
There's a reason:
But by the changing of the Colonels countenance,
The rolling of his eyes like angry Billows;
I fear the wind's not down yet, Ancient.

ANCIENT
Is the Duke well, Sir?

BOROSKIE
Not much unhealthy,
Only a little grudging of an Ague,
Which cannot last: he has heard, which makes him fearful,
And loth as yet to give your worth due welcome,
The sickness hath been somewhat hot i'th' Army,
Which happily may prove more doubt than danger,
And more his fear than fate; yet howsoever,
An honest care—

ARCHAS
Ye say right, and it shall be;
For though upon my life 'tis but a rumor,
A meer opinion, without faith or fear in't;
For Sir, I thank Heaven, we never stood more healthy,
Never more high and lusty; yet to satisfie,
We cannot be too curious, or too careful
Of what concerns his state, we'll draw away, Sir,
And lodge at further distance, and less danger.

BOROSKIE
It will be well.

ANCIENT
It will be very scurvy:
I smell it out, it stinks abominably,
Stir it no more.

BOROSKIE
The Duke, Sir, would have you too,
For a short day or two, retire to your own house,
Whither himself will come to visit ye,
And give ye thanks.

ARCHAS
I shall attend his pleasure.

ANCIENT
A trick, a lousie trick: so ho, a trick Boys.

ARCHAS
How now, what's that?

ANCIENT
I thought I had found a Hare, Sir,

But 'tis a Fox, an old Fox, shall we hunt him?

ARCHAS
No more such words.

BOROSKIE
The Souldier's grown too sawcy,
You must tie him straiter up.

ARCHAS
I do my best, Sir;
But men of free-born minds sometimes will flie out.

ANCIENT
May not we see the Duke?

BOROSKIE
Not at this time, Gentlemen,
Your General knows the cause.

ANCIENT
We have no Plague, Sir,
Unless it be in our pay, nor no Pox neither;
Or if we had, I hope that good old Courtier
Will not deny us place there.

PUTSKIE
Certain my Lord,
Considering what we are, and what we have done;
If not, what need ye may have, 'twould be better,
A great deal nobler, and taste honester
To use us with more sweetness; men that dig
And lash away their lives at the Carts tail,
Double our comforts; meat, and their Masters thanks too,
When they work well, they have; Men of our quality,
When they do well, and venture for't with valour,
Fight hard, lye hard, feed hard, when they come home, Sir,
And know these are deserving things, things worthy,
Can you then blame 'em if their minds a little
Be stir'd with glory? 'tis a pride becomes 'em,
A little season'd with ambition,
To be respected, reckon'd well, and honour'd
For what they have done: when to come home thus poorly,
And met with such unjointed joy, so looked on,
As if we had done no more but drest a Horse well;
So entertain'd, as if, I thank ye Gentlemen,
Take that to drink, had pow'r to please a Souldier?
Where be the shouts, the Bells rung out, the people?

The Prince himself?

ARCHAS
Peace: I perceive your eye, Sir,
Is fixt upon this Captain for his freedom,
And happily you find his tongue too forward;
As I am Master of the place I carry,
'Tis fit I think so too; but were I this man,
No stronger tie upon me, than the truth
And tongue to tell it, I should speak as he do's,
And think with modesty enough, such Saints
That daily thrust their loves and lives through hazards,
And fearless for their Countries peace, march hourly
Through all the doors of death, and know the darkest,
Should better be canoniz'd for their service:
What labour would these men neglect, what danger
Where honour is, though seated in a Billow,
Rising as high as Heaven, would not these Souldiers,
Like to so many Sea-gods charge up to it?
Do you see these swords? times Sythe was ne'er so sharp, Sir;
Nor ever at one harvest mow'd such handfuls:
Thoughts ne'er so sudden, nor belief so sure
When they are drawn, and were it not sometimes
I swim upon their angers to allay 'em,
And like a calm depress their fell intentions;
They are so deadly sure, nature would suffer—
And whose are all these glories? why, their Princes,
Their Countries, and their Friends? Alas, of all these,
And all the happy ends they bring, the blessings,
They only share the labours: A little joy then,
And outside of a welcome, at an upshot
Would not have done amiss, Sir; but howsoever
Between me and my duty, no crack, Sir,
Shall dare appear: I hope by my example
No discontent in them: without doubt Gentlemen,
The Duke will both look suddenly and truly
On your deserts: Methinks 'twere good they were paid, Sir.

BOROSKIE
They shall be immediately; I stay for money;
And any favour else—

ARCHAS
We are all bound to ye;
And so I take my leave, Sir; when the Duke pleases
To make me worthy of his eyes—

BOROSKIE

Which will be suddenly,
I know his good thoughts to ye.

ARCHAS
With all duty,
And all humility, I shall attend, Sir.

BOROSKIE
Once more you are welcome home: these shall be satisfied.

THEODORE
Be sure we be: and handsomly.

ARCHAS
Wait you on me, Sir.

THEODORE
And honestly: no jugling.

ARCHAS
Will ye come, Sir?

[Exit.

BOROSKIE
Pray do not doubt.

THEODORE
We are no Boys.

[Exit.

[Enter a **GENTLEMAN** and 2 or 3 with Mony.

BOROSKIE
Well Sir.

GENTLEMAN
Here's mony from the Duke, and't please your Lordship.

BOROSKIE
'Tis well.

GENTLEMAN
How sowre the Souldiers look?

BOROSKIE
Is't told?

GENTLEMAN
Yes, and for every company a double pay,
And the Dukes love to all.

ANCIENT
That's worth a Ducket.

BOROSKIE
You that be Officers, see it discharg'd then,
Why do not you take it up?

ANCIENT
'Tis too heavy:
'Body o'me, I have strain'd mine arm.

BOROSKIE
Do ye scorn it?

ANCIENT
Has your Lordship any dice about ye? sit round Gentlemen,
And come on seven for my share.

PUTSKIE
Do you think Sir,
This is the end we fight? can this durt draw us
To such a stupid tameness, that our service
Neglected, and look'd lamely on, and skew'd at
With a few honourable words, and this, is righted?
Have not we eyes and ears, to hear and see Sir,
And minds to understand the slights we carry?
I come home old, and full of hurts, men look on me
As if I had got 'em from a whore, and shun me;
I tell my griefs, and fear my wants, I am answer'd,
Alas 'tis pity! pray dine with me on Sunday:
These are the sores we are sick of, the minds maladies,
And can this cure 'em? you should have us'd us nobly,
And for our doing well, as well proclaim'd us
To the worlds eye, have shew'd and sainted us,
Then ye had paid us bravely: then we had shin'd Sir,
Not in this gilded stuff but in our glory:
You may take back your money.

GENTLEMAN
This I fear'd still.

BOROSKIE
Consider better Gentlemen.

ANCIENT
Thank your Lordship:
And now I'le put on my considering cap:
My Lord, that I am no Courtier, you may guess it
By having no sute to you for this mony:
For though I want, I want not this, nor shall not,
Whilst you want that civility to rank it
With those rights we expected; mony grows Sir,
And men must gather it, all is not put in one purse.
And that I am no Carter, I could never whistle yet:
But that I am a Souldier, and a Gentleman,
And a fine Gentleman, and't like your honour,
And a most pleasant companion: all you that are witty,
Come list to my ditty: come set in boyes,
With your Lordships patience.

[Song.

How do you like my Song, my Lord?

BOROSKIE
Even as I like your self, but 'twould be a great deal better,
You would prove a great deal wiser, and take this mony,
In your own phrase I speak now Sir, and 'tis very well
You have learn'd to sing; for since you prove so liberal,
To refuse such means as this, maintain your voice still,
'Twill prove your best friend.

ANCIENT
'Tis a singing age Sir,
A merry moon here now: I'le follow it:
Fidling, and fooling now, gains more than fighting.

BOROSKIE
What is't you blench at? what would you ask? speak freely.

SOULDIER
And so we dare: a triumph for the General,

PUTSKIE
And then an honour special to his vertue.

ANCIENT
That we may be prefer'd that have serv'd for it,
And cram'd up into favour like the worshipful,
At least upon the Cities charge made drunk
For one whole year; we have done 'em ten years service;

That we may enjoy our lechery without grudging,
And mine, or thine be nothing, all things equal,
And catch as catch may, be proclaim'd: that when we borrow,
And have no will to pay again, no Law
Lay hold upon us, nor no Court controule us.

BOROSKIE
Some of these may come to pass; the Duke may do 'em,
And no doubt will: the General will find too,
And so will you, if you but stay with patience: I have no power.

PUTSKIE
Nor will: come fellow Souldiers.

BOROSKIE
Pray be not so distrustfull.

PUTSKIE
There are waies yet,
And honest waies; we are not brought up Statues.

ANCIENT
If your Lordship
Have any silk stockings, that have holes i'th' heels,
Or ever an honourable Cassock that wants buttons,
I could have cur'd such maladies: your Lordships custome
And my good Ladies, if the bones want setting
In her old bodies—

BOROSKIE
This is disobedience.

ANCIENT
Eight pence a day, and hard Eggs.

PUTSKIE
Troop off Gentlemen,
Some Coin we have, whilst this lasts, or our credits,
We'l never sell our Generals worth for six-pence.
Ye are beholding to us.

ANCIENT
Fare ye well Sir,
And buy a pipe with that: do ye see this skarf Sir?
By this hand I'le cry Brooms in't, birchen Brooms Sir,
Before I eat one bit from your benevolence.
Now to our old occupations again.
By your leave Lord.

[Exeunt.

BOROSKIE
You will bite when ye are sharper; take up the mony.
This love I must remove, this fondness to him,
This tenderness of heart; I have lost my way else.
There is no sending man, they will not take it,
They are yet too full of pillage,
They'l dance for't ere't be long:
Come, bring it after.

[Enter **DUKE**.

DUKE
How now, refus'd their mony?

BOROSKIE
Very bravely,
And stand upon such terms 'tis terrible.

DUKE
Where's Archas?

BOROSKIE
He's retir'd Sir, to his house,
According to your pleasure, full of dutie
To outward shew: but what within—

DUKE
Refuse it?

BOROSKIE
Most confidently: 'tis not your revenues
Can feed them Sir, and yet they have found a General
That knows no ebbe of bountie: there they eat Sir,
And loath your invitations.

DUKE
'Tis not possible,
He's poor as they.

BOROSKIE
You'l find it otherwise.
Pray make your journey thither presently,
And as ye goe I'le open ye a wonder.
Good Sir this morning.

DUKE
Follow me, I'le doe it.

[Exeunt.

SCÆNA SECUNDA

Enter **OLYMPIA, ALINDA, BURRIS, PETESCA** and **GENTLEWOMAN**.

OLYMPIA
But do you think my Brother loves her?

BURRIS
Certain Madam,
He speaks much of her, and sometimes with wonder,
Oft wishes she were nobler born.

OLYMPIA
Do you think him honest?

BURRIS
Your Grace is nearer to his heart, than I am,
Upon my life I hold him so.

OLYMPIA
'Tis a poor wench,
I would not have her wrong'd: methinks my Brother—
But I must not give rules to his affections;
Yet if he weigh her worth—

BURRIS
You need not fear Madam.

OLYMPIA
I hope I shall not: Lord Burris
I love her well; I know not, there is something
Makes me bestow more than a care upon her:
I do not like that ring from him to her;
I mean to women of her way, such tokens
Rather appear as baits, than royal bounties:
I would not have it so.

BURRIS
You will not find it,
Upon my troth I think his most ambition
Is but to let the world know h'as a handsom Mistris:

Will your grace command me any service to him?

OLYMPIA
Remember all my duty.

BURRIS
Blessings crown ye:
What's your will Lady?

ALINDA
Any thing that's honest;
And if you think it fit, so poor a service,
Clad in a ragged vertue, may reach him,
I do beseech your Lordship speak it humbly.

BURRIS
Fair one I will: in the best phrase I have too,
And so I kiss your hand.

[Exit.

ALINDA
Your Lordships Servant.

OLYMPIA
Come hither wench, what art thou doing with that Ring?

ALINDA
I am looking on the posie, Madam.

OLYMPIA
What is't?

ALINDA
The Jewel's set within.

OLYMPIA
But where the joy wench,
When that invisible Jewel's lost? why dost thou smile so?
What unhappy meaning hast thou?

ALINDA
Nothing Madam,
But only thinking what strange spells these Rings have,
And how they work with some.

PUTSKIE
I fear with you too.

ALINDA
This could not cost above a Crown.

PETESCA
'Twill cost you
The shaving of your crown, if not the washing.

OLYMPIA
But he that sent it, makes the vertue greater;

ALINDA
I and the vice too Madam: goodness bless me:
How fit 'tis for my finger!

2ND WOMAN
No doubt you'l find too
A finger fit for you.

ALINDA
Sirrah, Petesca,
What wilt thou give me for the good that follows this?
But thou hast Rings enough, thou art provided:
Heigh ho, what must I doe now?

PETESCA
You'l be taught that,
The easiest part that e're you learn't, I warrant you.

ALINDA
Ay me, ay me.

PETESCA
You will divide too, shortly,
Your voice comes finely forward.

OLYMPIA
Come hither wanton,
Thou art not surely as thou saist.

ALINDA
I would not:
But sure there is a witchcraft in this Ring, Lady,
Lord how my heart leaps!

PETESCA
'Twill goe pit a pat shortly.

ALINDA
And now methinks a thousand of the Dukes shapes.

2ND WOMAN
Will no less serve ye?

ALINDA
In ten thousand smiles.

OLYMPIA
Heaven bless the wench.

ALINDA
With eyes that will not be deni'd to enter;
And such soft sweet embraces; take it from me,
I am undone else Madam: I'm lost else.

OLYMPIA
What ailes the girle?

ALINDA
How suddenly I'm alter'd!
And grown my self again! do not you feel it?

OLYMPIA
Wear that, and I'le wear this:
I'le try the strength on't.

ALINDA
How cold my bloud grows now!
Here's sacred vertue:
When I leave to honour this,
Every hour to pay a kiss,
When each morning I arise,
Or I forget a sacrifice:
When this figure in my faith,
And the pureness that it hath,
I pursue not with my will,
Nearer to arrive at still:
When I lose, or change this Jewel,
Flie me faith, and heaven be cruel.

OLYMPIA
You have half confirm'd me,
Keep but that way sure,
And what this charm can doe, let me endure.

[Exeunt.

SCÆNA TERTIA

Enter **ARCHAS**, **THEODORE**, 2 Daughters; **HONORA** and **VIOLA**.

ARCHAS
Carry your self discreetly, it concerns me,
The Duke's come in, none of your froward passions,
Nor no distasts to any: Prethee Theodor,
By my life, boy, 'twill ruine me.

THEODORE
I have done Sir,
So there be no foul play he brings along with him.

ARCHAS
What's that to you?
Let him bring what please him,
And whom, and how.

THEODORE
So they mean well—

ARCHAS
Is't fit you be a Judge sirrah?

THEODORE
'Tis fit I feel Sir.

ARCHAS
Get a banquet ready,
And trim your selves up handsomly.

THEODORE
To what end?
Do you mean to make 'em whores?
Hang up a sign then,
And set 'em out to Livery.

ARCHAS
Whose son art thou?

THEODORE
Yours Sir, I hope: but not of your disgraces.

ARCHAS

Full twenty thousand men I have commanded,
And all their minds, with this calm'd all their angers;
And shall a boy of mine own breed too, of mine own blood,
One crooked stick—

THEODORE
Pray take your way, and thrive in't,
I'le quit your house; if taint or black dishonour
Light on ye, 'tis your own, I have no share in't.
Yet if it do fall out so, as I fear it,
And partly find it too—

ARCHAS
Hast thou no reverence?
No dutie in thee?

THEODORE
This shall shew I obey ye:
I dare not stay: I would have shew'd my love too,
And that you ask as duty, with my life Sir,
Had you but thought me worthy of your hazards,
Which heaven preserve ye from, and keep the Duke too:
And there's an end of my wishes, God be with ye.

[Exit.

ARCHAS
Stubborn, yet full of that we all love, honesty.

[Enter **BURRIS**.

Lord Burris, where's the Duke?

BURRIS
In the great chamber Sir,
And there stayes till he see you, ye 'have a fine house here.

ARCHAS
A poor contented lodge, unfit for his presence,
Yet all the joy it hath.

BURRIS
I hope a great one, and for your good, brave Sir.

ARCHAS
I thank ye Lord:
And now my service to the Duke.

BURRIS
I'le wait on ye.

[Exeunt.

[Enter **DUKE**, **BOROSKIE**, **GENTLEMAN** and **ATTENDANTS**.

DUKE
May this be credited?

BOROSKIE
Disgrace me else,
And never more with favour look upon me.

DUKE
It seems impossible.

BOROSKIE
It cannot chuse Sir,
Till your own eyes behold it; but that it is so,
And that by this means the too haughtie Souldier
Has been so cramm'd and fed, he cares not for ye;
Believe, or let me perish: Let your eyes
As you observe the house, but where I point it,
Make stay, and take a view, and then you have found it.

[Enter **ARCHAS**, **BURRIS**, **TWO DAUGHTERS** and **SERVANT**.

DUKE
I'le follow your direction: welcome Archas,
You are welcome home brave Lord, we are come to visit ye,
And thank ye for your service.

ARCHAS
'Twas so poor Sir,
In true respect of what I owe your Highness,
It merits nothing.

DUKE
Are these fair ones yours, Lord?

ARCHAS
Their Mother made me think so Sir.

DUKE
Stand up Ladies:
Beshrew my heart they are fair ones; methinks fitter
The lustre of the Court, than thus live darken'd:

I would see your house Lord Archas, it appears to me
A handsom pile.

ARCHAS
'Tis neat but no great structure;
I'le be your Graces guide, give me the keyes there.

DUKE
Lead on, we'l follow ye: begin with the Gallery,
I think that's one.

ARCHAS
'Tis so, and't please ye, Sir,
The rest above are lodgings all.

DUKE
Go on, Sir.

[Exeunt.

SCÆNA QUARTA

Enter **THEODORE**, **PUKSKIE** and **ANCIENT**.

PUTSKIE
The Duke gone thither, do you say?

THEODORE
Yes marry do I,
And all the Ducklings too; but what they'll do there—

PUTSKIE
I hope they'll crown his service.

THEODORE
With a Custard;
This is no weather for rewards: they crown his service?
Rather they go to shave his Crown: I was rated
As if I had been a Dog had worried Sheep, out of doors,
For making but a doubt.

PUTSKIE
They must now grace him.

THEODORE
Mark but the end.

ANCIENT
I am sure they should reward him, they cannot want him.

THEODORE
They that want honesty, want any thing.

PUTSKIE
The Duke is so noble in his own thoughts.

THEODORE
That I grant ye,
If those might only sway him: but 'tis most certain,
So many new born Flies his light gave life to,
Buzze in his beams, Flesh-flies, and Butterflies,
Hornets, and humming Scarabs, that not one honey Bee
That's loaden with true labour, and brings home
Encrease and Credit, can 'scape rifling,
And what she sucks for sweet, they turn to bitterness.

ANCIENT
Shall we go see what they do, and talk our mind to 'em?

PUTSKIE
That we have done too much, and to no purpose.

ANCIENT
Shall we be hang'd for him?
I have a great mind to be hang'd now
For doing some brave thing for him; a worse end will take me,
And for an action of no worth; not honour him?
Upon my Conscience, even the Devil, the very Devil
(Not to belie him) thinks him an honest man,
I am sure he has sent him souls any time these twenty years,
Able to furnish all his Fish-markets.

THEODORE
Leave thy talking,
And come, let's go to dinner and drink to him,
We shall hear more ere supper time: if he be honour'd,
He has deserv'd it well, and we shall fight for't:
If he be ruin'd, so, we know the worst then,
And for my self, I'll meet it.

PUTSKIE
I ne'r fear it.

[Exeunt.

SCÆNA QUINTA

Enter **DUKE**, **ARCHAS**, **BOROSKIE**, **BURRIS**, **GENTLEMEN** and **ATTENDANTS**.

DUKE
They are handsome rooms all, well contriv'd and fitted,
Full of convenience, the prospect's excellent.

ARCHAS
Now will your Grace pass down, and do me but the honour
To taste a Countrey Banquet?

DUKE
What room's that?
I would see all now; what conveyance has it?
I see you have kept the best part yet; pray open it.

ARCHAS
Ha! I misdoubted this: 'tis of no receipt, Sir,
For your eyes most unfit—

DUKE
I long to see it,
Because I would judge of the whole piece: some excellent painting,
Or some rare spoils you would keep to entertain me
Another time, I know.

ARCHAS
In troth there is not,
Nor any thing worth your sight; below I have
Some Fountains, and some Ponds.

DUKE
I would see this now.

ARCHAS
Boroskie, thou art a Knave; it contains nothing
But rubbish from the other rooms and unnecessaries:
Will't please you see a strange Clock?

DUKE
This or nothing: [Little Trunk ready.
Why should you bar it up thus with defences
Above the rest, unless it contain'd something
More excellent, and curious of keeping?

Open't, for I will see it.

ARCHAS
The Keys are lost, Sir:
Does your Grace think if it were fit for you,
I could be so unmannerly?

DUKE
I will see it, and either shew it—

ARCHAS
Good Sir—

DUKE
Thank ye, Archas,
You shew your love abundantly,
Do I use to entreat thus? force it open.

BURRIS
That were inhospitable; you are his Guest, Sir,
And with his greatest joy, to entertain ye.

DUKE
Hold thy peace, Fool; will ye open it?

ARCHAS
Sir, I cannot.
I must not if I could.

DUKE
Go, break it open.

ARCHAS
I must withstand that force: Be not too rash, Gentlemen.

DUKE
Unarm him first, then if he be not obstinate
Preserve his life.

ARCHAS
I thank your Grace, I take it;
And now take you the Keys, go in, and see, Sir;
There feed your eyes with wonder, and thank that Traytor,
That thing that sells his faith for favour.

[Exit **DUKE**.

BURRIS

Sir, what moves ye?

ARCHAS
I have kept mine pure: Lord Burris, there's a Judas,
That for a smile will sell ye all: a Gentleman?
The Devil has more truth, and has maintain'd it;
A Whores heart more belief in't.

[Enter **DUKE**.

DUKE
What's all this, Archas?
I cannot blame you to conceal it so,
This most inestimable Treasure.

ARCHAS
Yours Sir.

DUKE
Nor do I wonder now the Souldier sleights me.

ARCHAS
Be not deceiv'd; he has had no favour here, Sir,
Nor had you known this now, but for that Pick-thank,
The lost man in his faith, he has reveal'd it,
To suck a little honey from ye has betray'd it.
I swear he smiles upon me, and forsworn too,
Thou crackt, uncurrant Lord: I'll tell ye all, Sir:
Your Sire, before his death, knowing your temper,
To be as bounteous as the air, and open,
As flowing as the Sea to all that follow'd ye,
Your great mind fit for War and Glory, thriftily
Like a great Husband to preserve your actions,
Collected all this treasure; to our trusts,
To mine I mean, and to that long-tongu'd Lord's there,
He gave the knowledg and the charge of all this,
Upon his death-Bed too: And on the Sacrament
He swore us thus, never to let this Treasure
Part from our secret keepings, till no hope
Of Subject could relieve ye, all your own wasted,
No help of those that lov'd ye could supply ye,
And then some great exploit a foot; my honesty
I would have kept till I had made this useful;
I shew'd it, and I stood it to the tempest,
And useful to the end 'twas left: I am cozen'd,
And so are you too, if you spend this vainly;
This Worm that crept into ye has abus'd ye,
Abus'd your fathers care, abus'd his Faith too:

Nor can this mass of money make him man more,
A flea'd Dog has more soul, an Ape more honesty;
All mine ye have amongst it, farewel that,
I cannot part with't nobler; my heart's clear,
My Conscience smooth as that, no rub upon't:
But O thy Hell!

BOROSKIE
I seek no Heaven from you, Sir.

ARCHAS
Thy gnawing Hell, Boroskey, it will find thee:
Would ye heap Coals upon his head has wrong'd ye,
Has ruin'd your estate? give him this money,
Melt it into his mouth.

DUKE
What little Trunk's that?
That there o'th' top, that's lockt?

BOROSKIE
You'll find it rich, Sir,
Richer I think than all.

ARCHAS
You were not covetous,
Nor wont to weave your thoughts with such a courseness;
Pray rack not Honesty.

BOROSKIE
Be sure you see it.

DUKE
Bring out the Trunk.

[Enter with the Trunk.

ARCHAS
You'll find that treasure too,
All I have left me now.

DUKE
What's this, a poor Gown?
And this a piece of Seneca?

ARCHAS
Yes sure, Sir,
More worth than all your Gold, yet ye have enough on't,

And of a Mine far purer, and more precious;
This sells no friends, nor searches into counsels,
And yet all counsel, and all friends live here, Sir;
Betrays no Faith, yet handles all that's trusty:
Will't please you leave me this?

DUKE
With all my heart, Sir.

ARCHAS
What says your Lordship to't?

BOROSKIE
I dare not rob ye.

ARCHAS
Poor miserable men, you have rob'd your selves both;
This Gown, and this unvalu'd Treasure, your brave Father,
Found me a Child at School with, in his progress.
Where such a love he took to some few answers,
Unhappy Boyish toys hit in my head then,
That suddenly I made him, thus as I was,
(For here was all the Wealth I brought his Highness)
He carried me to Court, there bred me up,
Bestow'd his favours on me, taught me the Arms first,
With those an honest mind; I serv'd him truly,
And where he gave me trust, I think I fail'd not;
Let the World speak: I humbly thank your Highness,
You have done more, and nobler, eas'd mine age, Sir;
And to this care a fair Quietus given,
Now to my Book again.

DUKE
You have your wish, Sir,
Let some bring off the treasure.

BOROSKIE
Some is his, Sir.

ARCHAS
None, none, a poor unworthy reaper,
The Harvest is his Graces.

DUKE
Thank you, Archas.

ARCHAS
But will not you repent, Lord? when this is gone

Where will your Lordship?—

BOROSKIE
Pray take you no care, Sir.

ARCHAS
Does your Grace like my House?

DUKE
Wondrous well, Archas,
You have made me richly welcome.

ARCHAS
I did my best, Sir.
Is there any thing else may please your Grace?

DUKE
Your Daughters
I had forgot, send them to Court.

ARCHAS
How's that, Sir?

DUKE
I said your Daughters; see it done: I'll have 'em
Attend my Sister, Archas.

ARCHAS
Thank your Highness.

DUKE
And suddenly.

[Exit.

ARCHAS
Through all the ways I dare,
I'll serve your temper, though you try me far.

[Exit.

ACTUS TERTIUS

SCÆNA PRIMA

Enter **THEODORE**, **PUTSKIE**, **ANCIENT** and **SERVANT**.

THEODORE
I wonder we hear no news.

PUTSKIE
Here's your fathers servant,
He comes in haste too, now we shall know all, Sir.

THEODORE
How now?

SERVANT
I am glad I have met you, Sir; your father
Intreats you presently make haste unto him.

THEODORE
What news?

SERVANT
None of the best, Sir, I am asham'd to tell it,
Pray ask no more.

THEODORE
Did not I tell ye, Gentlemen?
Did not I prophesie? he's undone then.

SERVANT
Not so, Sir, but as near it—

PUTSKIE
There's no help now;
The Army's scatter'd all, through discontent,
Not to be rallied up in haste to help this.

ANCIENT
Plague of the Devil; have ye watch'd your seasons?
We shall watch you ere long.

THEODORE
Farewel, there's no cure,
We must endure all now: I know what I'll do.

[Exeunt **THEODORE** and **SERVANT**.

PUTSKIE
Nay, there's no striving, they have a hand upon us,
A heavy and a hard one.

ANCIENT
Now I have it,
We have yet some Gentlemen, some Boys of mettle,
(What, are we bob'd thus still, colted, and carted?)
And one mad trick we'll have to shame these Vipers;
Shall I bless 'em?

PUTSKIE
Farewel; I have thought my way too.

[Exit.

ANCIENT
Were never such rare Cries in Christendome,
As Mosco shall afford: we'll live by fooling
Now fighting's gone, and they shall find and feel it.

[Exit.

SCÆNA SECUNDA

Enter **ARCHAS**, **HONORA** and **VIOLA**.

ARCHAS
No more, it must be so; do you think I would send ye,
Your father and your friend—

VIOLA
Pray Sir, be good to us,
Alas, we know no Court, nor seek that knowledge;
We are content with harmless things at home,
Children of your content, bred up in quiet,
Only to know our selves, to seek a Wisedome
From that we understand, easie and honest;
To make our actions worthy of your Honour,
Their ends as innocent as we begot 'em;
What shall we look for Sir, what shall we learn there,
That this more private sweetness cannot teach us?
Vertue was never built upon ambition,
Nor the Souls Beauties bred out of Bravery:
What a terrible Father would you seem to us,
Now you have moulded us, and wrought our tempers
To easie and obedient ways, uncrooked,
Where the fair mind can never lose nor loiter,
Now to divert our Natures, now to stem us
Roughly against the tide of all this treasure?

Would ye have us proud? 'tis sooner bred than buried;
Wickedly proud? for such things dwell at Court, Sir.

HONORA
Would ye have your Children learn to forget their father,
And when he dies dance on his Monument?
Shall we seek Vertue in a Sattin Gown;
Embroider'd Vertue? Faith in a well-curl'd Feather?
And set our Credits to the tune of green sleeves?
This may be done; and if you like, it shall be.
You should have sent us thither when we were younger,
Our maiden-heads at a higher rate; our Innocence
Able to make a Mart indeed: we are now too old, Sir,
Perhaps they'll think too cunning too, and slight us;
Besides, we are altogether unprovided,
Unfurnisht utterly of the rules should guide us:
This Lord comes, licks his hand, and protests to me;
Compares my Beauty to a thousand fine things;
Mountains, and Fountains, Trees, and Stars, and Goblins;
Now have not I the faith for to believe him;
He offers me the honourable courtesie,
To lye with me all night, what a misery is this?
I am bred up so foolishly, alas, I dare not,
And how madly these things will shew there.

ARCHAS
I send ye not,
Like parts infected, to draw more corruption;
Like Spiders to grow great, with growing evil:
With your own Vertues season'd, and my prayers,
The Card of goodness in your minds, that shows ye
When ye sail false; the needle toucht with honour,
That through the blackest storms, still points at happiness;
Your Bodies the tall barks, rib'd round with goodness,
Your Heavenly Souls the Pilots, thus I send you;
Thus I prepare your Voyage; sound before ye,
And ever as you sail through this Worlds Vanity,
Discover Sholes, Rocks, Quicksands, cry out to ye,
Like a good Master tack about for Honour:
The Court is Vertue's School, at least it should be;
Nearer the Sun the Mine lies, the metal's purer:
Be it granted, if the spring be once infected,
Those Branches that flow from him must run muddy;
Say you find some Sins there, and those no small ones,
And they like lazie fits begin to shake ye:
Say they affect your strengths, my happy Children,
Great things through greatest hazards are atchiev'd still,
And then they shine, then goodness has his glory,

His Crown fast rivetted, then time moves under,
Where, through the mist of errors, like the Sun,
Through thick and pitchy Clouds, he breaks out nobly.

HONORA
I thank you Sir, you have made me half a Souldier,
I will to Court most willingly, most fondly.
And if there be such stirring things amongst 'em,
Such Travellers into Virginia
As Fame reports, if they can win me, take me;
I think I have a close Ward, and a sure one;
An honest mind I hope, 'tis petticoat-proof,
Chain-proof, and Jewel-proof; I know 'tis Gold-proof,
A Coach and four Horses cannot draw me from it:
As for your handsome Faces, and filed Tongues,
Curl'd Millers heads, I have another word for them,
And yet I'll flatter too, as fast as they do,
And lye, but not as lewdly; Come, be valiant, Sister,
She that dares not stand the push o'th' Court, dares nothing,
And yet come off ungraced: Sir, like you,
We both affect great dangers now, and the World shall see
All glory lies not in Mans Victorie.

ARCHAS
Mine own Honora.

VIOLA
I am very fearful,
Would I were stronger built: you would have me honest?

ARCHAS
Or not at all my Viola.

VIOLA
I'll think on't,
For 'tis no easie promise, and live there:
Do you think we shall do well?

HONORA
Why, what should aile us?

VIOLA
Certain they'll tempt us strongly; beside the glory
Which Women may affect, they are handsom Gentlemen,
Every part speaks: nor is it one denial,
Nor two, nor ten; from every look we give 'em,
They'll frame a hope; even from our prayers, promises.

HONORA
Let 'em feed so, and be fat; there is no fear, wench,
If thou beest fast to thy self.

VIOLA
I hope I shall be;
And your example will work more.

[Enter **THEODORE**.

HONORA
Thou shalt not want it.

THEODORE
How do you, Sir? can you lend a man an Angel?
I hear you let out money.

ARCHAS
Very well, Sir,
You are pleasantly dispos'd: I am glad to see it.
Can you lend me your patience, and be rul'd by me?

THEODORE
Is't come to patience now?

ARCHAS
Is't not a Vertue?

THEODORE
I know not: I ne'r found it so.

ARCHAS
That's because
Thy anger ever knows, and not thy judgment.

THEODORE
I know you have been rifl'd.

ARCHAS
Nothing less, Boy;
Lord, what opinions these vain People publish!
Rifl'd of what?

THEODORE
Study your Vertue, Patience,
It may get Mustard to your Meat. Why in such haste, Sir,
Sent ye for me?

ARCHAS
For this end only, Theodore,
To wait upon your Sisters to the Court;
I am commanded they live there.

THEODORE
To th' Court, Sir?

ARCHAS
To th' Court I say.

THEODORE
And must I wait upon 'em?

ARCHAS
Yes, 'tis most fit you should, you are their Brother.

THEODORE
Is this the business? I had thought your mind, Sir,
Had been set forward on some noble action,
Something had truly stir'd ye. To th' Court with these?
Why, they are your Daughters, Sir.

ARCHAS
All this I know, Sir.

THEODORE
The good old Woman on a Bed he threw:
To th' Court?

ARCHAS
Thou art mad.

THEODORE
Nor drunk as you are:
Drunk with your duty, Sir: do you call it duty?
A pox of duty, what can these do there?
What should they do? Can ye look Babies, Sisters,
In the young Gallants eyes, and twirl their Band-strings?
Can ye ride out to air your selves? Pray Sir,
Be serious with me, do you speak this truly?

ARCHAS
Why, didst thou never hear of Women
Yet at Court, Boy?

THEODORE
Yes, and good Women too, very good Women,

Excellent honest Women: but are you sure, Sir,
That these will prove so?

HONORA
There's the danger, Brother.

THEODORE
God-a-mercy Wench, thou hast a grudging of it.

ARCHAS
Now be you serious, Sir, and observe what I say,
Do it, and do it handsomly; go with 'em.

THEODORE
With all my heart, Sir; I am in no fault now;
If they be thought Whores for being in my Company;
Pray write upon their Backs, they are my Sisters,
And where I shall deliver 'em.

ARCHAS
Ye are wondrous jocund,
But prithee tell me, art thou so lewd a Fellow?
I never knew thee fail a truth.

THEODORE
I am a Souldier,
And spell you what that means.

ARCHAS
A Souldier?
What dost thou make of me?

THEODORE
Your Palate's down, Sir.

ARCHAS
I thank ye, Sir.

THEODORE
Come, shall we to this matter?
You will to Court?

HONORA
If you will please to honour us.

THEODORE
I'll honour ye, I warrant; I'll set ye off
With such a lustre, Wenches; alas poor Viola,

Thou art a fool, thou criest for eating white bread:
Be a good Huswife of thy tears, and save 'em,
Thou wilt have time enough to shed 'em, Sister.
Do you weep too? nay, then I'll fool no more.
Come worthy Sisters, since it must be so,
And since he thinks it fit to try your Vertues,
Be you as strong to truth, as I to guard ye,
And this old Gentleman shall have joy of ye.

[Exeunt.

SCÆNA TERTIA

Enter **DUKE** and **BURRIS**.

DUKE
Burris take you ten thousand of those Crowns,
And those two Chains of Pearl they hold the richest,
I give 'em ye.

BURRIS
I humbly thank your Grace;
And may your great example work in me
That noble Charity to men more worthy,
And of more wants.

DUKE
You bear a good mind, Burris;
Take twenty thousand now: be not so modest,
It shall be so, I give 'em: go, there's my ring for't.

BURRIS
Heaven bless your Highness ever.

[Exit.

DUKE
You are honest.

[Enter **ALINDA** and **PUTSKIE** at door.

PUTSKIE
They're coming now to Court, as fair as vertue:
Two brighter Stars ne'er rose here.

ALINDA

Peace, I have it,
And what my Art can do; the Duke—

PUTSKIE
I am gone,
Remember.

[Exit.

ALINDA
I am counsell'd to the full, Sir.

DUKE
My pretty Mistris, whither lyes your business?
How kindly I should take this, were it to me now?

ALINDA
I must confess immediately to your Grace,
At this time.

DUKE
You have no address, I do believe ye,
I would ye had.

ALINDA
'Twere too much boldness, Sir,
Upon so little knowledge, less deserving.

DUKE
You'll make a perfect Courtier.

ALINDA
A very poor one.

DUKE
A very fair one, sweet; come hither to me.
What killing eyes this Wench has! in his glory
Not the bright Sun, when the Sirian Star reigns,
Shines half so fiery.

ALINDA
Why does your Grace so view me?
Nothing but common handsomness dwells here, Sir,
Scarce that: your Grace is pleas'd to mock my meanness.

DUKE
Thou shalt not go: I do not lie unto thee,
In my eye thou appear'st—

ALINDA
Dim not the sight, Sir,
I am too dull an object.

DUKE
Canst thou love me?
Canst thou love him will honour thee?

ALINDA
I can love,
And love as you do too: but 'twill not shew well:
Or if it do shew here where all light lustres,
Tinsel affections make a glorious glistering,
'Twill halt i'th' handsom way.

DUKE
Are ye so cunning?
Dost think I love not truly?

ALINDA
No, ye cannot,
You never travel'd that way yet: pray pardon me,
I prate so boldly to you.

DUKE
There's no harm done:
But what's your reason, sweet?

ALINDA
I would tell your Grace,
But happily—

DUKE
It shall be pleasing to me.

ALINDA
I should love you again, and then you would hate me.
With all my service I should follow ye,
And through all dangers.

DUKE
This would more provoke me,
More make me see thy worths,
More make me meet 'em.

ALINDA
You should do so, if ye did well and truly:

But though ye be a Prince, and have power in ye,
Power of example too, ye have fail'd and falter'd.

DUKE
Give me example where?

ALINDA
You had a Mistris,
Oh Heaven, so bright, so brave a dame, so lovely,
In all her life so true!

DUKE
A Mistris?

ALINDA
That serv'd you with that constancy, that care,
That lov'd your will, and woo'd it too.

DUKE
What Mistris?

ALINDA
That nurs'd your honour up, held fast your vertue,
And when she kist encreas'd, not stole your goodness.

DUKE
And I neglected her?

ALINDA
Lost her, forsook her,
Wantonly flung her off.

DUKE
What was her name?

ALINDA
Her name as lovely as her self, as noble,
And in it all that's excellent.

DUKE
What was it?

ALINDA
Her name was Beau-desert:
Do you know her now, Sir?

DUKE
Beau-desert? I do not remember—

ALINDA
I know you do not;
Yet she has a plainer name; Lord Archas service;
Do you yet remember her? there was a Mistris
Fairer than Woman, far fonder to you, Sir,
Than Mothers to their first-born joyes: Can you love?
Dare you profess that truth to me a stranger,
A thing of no regard, no name, no lustre,
When your most noble love you have neglected,
A beauty all the world would woo and honour?
Would you have me credit this? think you can love me,
And hold ye constant, when I have read this story?
Is't possible you should ever favour me,
To a slight pleasure prove a friend, and fast too,
When, where you were most ty'd, most bound to benefit,
Bound by the chains of honesty and honour,
You have broke and boldly too? I am a weak one,
Arm'd only with my fears: I beseech your Grace
Tempt me no further.

DUKE
Who taught you this Lesson?

ALINDA
Woful experience, Sir: if you seek a fair one,
Worthy your love, if yet you have that perfect,
Two Daughters of his ruin'd vertue now
Arrive at Court, excellent fair indeed, Sir,
But this will be the Plague on't, they're excellent honest.

[Enter **OLYMPIA** and **PETESCA** privately.

DUKE
I love thy face.

ALINDA
Upon my life ye cannot:
I do not love it my self, Sir, 'tis a lewd one,
So truly ill Art cannot mend it; but if 'twere handsome,
At least if I thought so, you should hear me talk, Sir,
In a new strain; and though ye are a Prince,
Make ye Petition to me too, and wait my answers;
Yet o' my Conscience I should pity ye,
After some ten years siege.

DUKE
Prethee do now.

ALINDA
What would ye do?

DUKE
Why I would lye with ye.

ALINDA
I do not think ye would.

DUKE
In troth I would Wench.
Here, take this Jewel.

ALINDA
Out upon't, that's scurvy.
Nay, if we do, sure we'll do for good fellowship,
For pure love, or nothing: thus you shall be sure, Sir,
You shall not pay too dear for't.

DUKE
Sure I cannot.

ALINDA
By'r Lady but ye may: when ye have found me able
To do your work well, ye may pay my wages.

PETESCA
Why does your Grace start back?

OLYMPIA
I ha' seen that shakes me:
Chills all my bloud: O where is faith or goodness?
Alinda thou art false, false, false thou fair one,
Wickedness false; and (wo is me) I see it.
For ever false.

PETESCA
I am glad 't has taken thus right.

[Exeunt.

ALINDA
I'le go ask my Lady, Sir.

DUKE
What?

ALINDA
Whether I shall lye with ye, or no: If I find her willing—
For look ye Sir, I have sworn, while I am in her service—
('Twas a rash Oath I must confess.)

DUKE
Thou mockst me.

ALINDA
Why, would ye lye with me, if I were willing?
Would you abuse my weakness?

DUKE
I would piece it,
And make it stronger.

ALINDA
I humbly thank your highness,
When you piece me, you must piece me to my Coffin:
When you have got my Maiden-head, I take it,
'Tis not an inch of an Apes tail will restore it,
I love ye, and I honour ye, but this way
I'le neither love nor serve ye.
Heaven change your mind, Sir.

[Exit.

DUKE
And thine too:
For it must be chang'd, it shall be.

[Exit.

SCÆNA QUARTA

Enter **BOROSKIE**, **BURRIS**, **THEODORE**, **VIOLA** and **HONORA**.

BOROSKIE
They are goodly Gentlewomen.

BURRIS
They are,
Wondrous sweet Women both.

THEODORE
Does your Lordship like 'em?

They are my Sisters, Sir; good lusty Lasses,
They'll do their labour well, I warrant ye,
You'll find no Bed-straw here, Sir.

HONORA
Thank ye Brother.

THEODORE
This is not so strongly built: but she is good mettle,
Of a good stirring strain too: she goes tith, Sir.

[Enter **TWO GENTLEMEN**.

Here they be, Gentlemen, must make ye merry,
The toyes you wot of: do you like their complexions?
They be no Moors: what think ye of this hand, Gentlemen?
Here's a white Altar for your sacrifice:
A thousand kisses here. Nay, keep off yet Gentlemen,
Let's start first, and have fair play: what would ye give now
To turn the Globe up, and find the rich Moluccas?
To pass the straights? here (do ye itch) by St Nicholas,
Here's that will make ye scratch and claw,
Claw my fine Gentlemen, move ye in divers sorts:
Pray ye let me request ye, to forget
To say your prayers, whilest these are Courtiers;
Or if ye needs will think of Heaven, let it be no higher
Than their eyes.

BOROSKIE
How will ye have 'em bestow'd, Sir?

THEODORE
Even how your Lordship please,
So you do not bake 'em.

BOROSKIE
Bake 'em?

THEODORE
They are too high a meat that way, they run to gelly.
But if you'll have 'em for your own diet, take my counsel,
Stew 'em between two Feather-beds.

BURRIS
Please you Colonel
To let 'em wait upon the Princess?

THEODORE

Yes, Sir,
And thank your honour too: but then happily,
These noble Gentlemen shall have no access to 'em,
And to have 'em buy new Cloaths, study new faces,
And keep a stinking stir with themselves for nothing,
'Twill not be well i'faith: they have kept their bodies,
And been at charge for Bathes: do you see that shirt there?
Weigh but the moral meaning, 'twill be grievous:
Alas, I brought 'em to delight these Gentlemen,
I weigh their wants by mine: I brought 'em wholesome,
Wholesome, and young my Lord, and two such blessings
They will not light upon again in ten years.

BOROSKIE
'Tis fit they wait upon her.

THEODORE
They are fit for any thing:
They'll wait upon a man, they are not bashful,
Carry his Cloak, or unty his points, or any thing,
Drink drunk, and take Tobacco; the familiar'st fools—
This wench will leap over Stools too, and sound a Trumpet,
Wrastle, and pitch the Bar; they are finely brought up.

BOROSKIE
Ladies, ye are bound to your Brother,
And have much cause to thank him:
I'le ease ye of this charge, and to the Princess,
So please you, I'le attend 'em.

THEODORE
Thank your Lordship:
If there be e're a private corner as ye go, Sir,
A foolish lobbie out o'th' way, make danger,
Try what they are, try—

BOROSKIE
Ye are a merry Gentleman.

THEODORE
I would fain be your honours kinsman.

BOROSKIE
Ye are too curst, Sir.

THEODORE
Farewel wenches, keep close your ports, y'are washt else.

HONORA
Brother, bestow your fears where they are needful.

[Exit **BOROSKIE**, **HONORA** and **VIOLA**.

THEODORE
Honor thy name is, and I hope thy Nature.
Go after, Gentlemen, go, get a snatch if you can,
Yond' old Erra Pater will never please 'em.
Alas I brought 'em for you, but see the luck on't,
I swear I meant as honestly toward ye—
Nay do not cry good Gentlemen: a little counsel
Will do no harm: they'll walk abroad i'th' Evenings,
Ye may surprize 'em easily, they wear no Pistols.
Set down your minds in Metre, flowing Metre,
And get some good old linnen Woman to deliver it,
That has the trick on't: you cannot fail:
Farewel Gentlemen.

[Exeunt **GENTLEMEN**.

BURRIS
You have frighted off these flesh-flies.

THEODORE
Flesh-flies indeed my Lord.

[Enter a **SERVANT**.

And it must be very stinking flesh they will not seize on.

SERVANT
Your Lordship bid me bring this Casket.

BURRIS
Yes, Good Colonel
Commend me to your worthy Father, and as a pledge
He ever holds my love, and service to him,
Deliver him this poor, but hearty token,
And where I may be his—

THEODORE
Ye are too noble;
A wonder here my Lord, that dare be honest,
When all men hold it vitious: I shall deliver it,
And with it your most noble love. Your servant.

[Exit **BURRIS**.

Were there but two more such at Court, 'twere Sainted,
This will buy Brawn this Christmas yet, and Muscadine.

[Exit.

SCÆNA QUINTA

Enter **ANCIENT**, crying Brooms, and after him severally, four **SOULDIERS**, crying other things. **BOROSKIE** and **GENTLEMEN**, over the Stage observing them.

I. SONG.

ANCIENT
Broom, Broom, the bonnie Broom,
Come buy my Birchen Broom,
I'th' Wars we have no more room,
Buy all my bonnie Broom,
For a kiss take two;
If those will not do,
For a little, little pleasure,
Take all my whole treasure:
If all these will not do't,
Take the Broom-man to boot.
Broom, Broom, the bonnie Broom.

II. SONG.

1ST SOULDIER
The Wars are done and gone,
And Souldiers now neglected, Pedlers are,
Come Maidens, come alone,
For I can show you handsome, handsome ware;
Powders for, for the head,
And drinks for your bed,
To make ye blith and bonney.
As well in the night we Souldiers can fight,
And please a young wench as any.

2ND SOULDIER
I have fine Potato's,
Ripe Potato's.

III. SONG.

3RD SOULDIER

Will ye buy any Honesty, come away,
I sell it openly by day,
I bring no forced light, nor no Candle
To cozen ye; come buy and handle:
This will shew the great man good,
The Tradesman where he swears and lyes,
Each Lady of a noble bloud,
The City dame to rule her eyes:
Ye are rich men now: come buy, and then
I'le make ye richer, honest men.

IV. SONG.

4ᵀᴴ SOULDIER
Have ye any crackt maiden-heads, to new leach or mend?
Have ye any old maiden-heads to sell or to change?
Bring 'em to me with a little pretty gin,
I'le clout 'em, I'le mend 'em, I'le knock in a pin,
Shall make 'em as good maids agen,
As ever they have been.

BOROSKIE
What means all this, why do y'sell Brooms Ancient?
Is it in wantonness, or want?

ANCIENT
The only reason is,
To sweep your Lordships conscience: here's one for the nonce.
Gape Sir, you have swallowed many a goodlier matter—
The only casting for a crazie conscience.

3ᴿᴰ SOULDIER
Will your Lordship buy any honestie? 'twill be worth your mony.

BOROSKIE
How is this?

3ᴿᴰ SOULDIER
Honestie my Lord, 'tis here in a quill.

ANCIENT
Take heed you open it not, for 'tis so subtle,
The least puffe of wind will blow it out o'th' Kingdom.

2ᴺᴰ SOULDIER
Will your Lordship please to taste a fine Potato?
'Twill advance your wither'd state.

ANCIENT
Fill your honour full of most noble itches,
And make Jack dance in your Lordships breeches.

1ST SOULDIER
If your Daughters on their beds.
Have bow'd, or crackt their maiden-heads;
If in a Coach with two much tumbling,
They chance to crie, fie, fo, what fumbling;
If her foot slip, and down fall she,
And break her leg 'bove the knee,
The one and thirtieth of Februarie let this be ta'ne,
And they shall be arrant maids again.

BOROSKIE
Ye are brave Souldiers; keep your wantonness,
A winter will come on to shake this wilfulness.
Disport your selves, and when you want your mony—

[Exit.

ANCIENT
Broom, Broom, &c.

[Exeunt Singing.

SCÆNA SEXTA

Enter **ALINDA**, **HONORA**, **VIOLA**.

ALINDA
You must not be so fearfull, little one,
Nor Lady you so sad, you will ne're make Courtiers
With these dull sullen thoughts; this place is pleasure,
Preserv'd to that use, so inhabited;
And those that live here, live delightfull, joyfull:
These are the Gardens of Adonis, Ladies,
Where all sweets to their free and noble uses,
Grow ever young and courted.

HONORA
Bless me Heaven,
Can things of her years arrive at these rudiments?
By your leave fair Gentlewoman, how long have you been here?

ALINDA

Faith much about a week.

HONORA
You have studied hard,
And by my faith arriv'd at a great knowledge.

VIOLA
Were not you bashfull at first?

ALINDA
I, I, for an hour or two:
But when I saw people laugh'd at me for it,
And thought it a dull breeding—

HONORA
You are govern'd here then
Much after the mens opinions.

ALINDA
Ever Lady.

HONORA
And what they think is honourable.—

ALINDA
Most precisely
We follow with all faith.

HONORA
A goodly Catechisme.

VIOLA
But bashfull for an hour or two?

ALINDA
Faith to say true,
I do not think I was so long: for look ye,
'Tis to no end here, put on what shape ye will,
And soure your self with ne're so much austeritie,
You shall be courted in the same, and won too,
'Tis but some two hours more; and so much time lost,
Which we hold pretious here: In so much time now
As I have told you this, you may lose a Servant,
Your age, nor all your Art can e're recover.
Catch me occasion as she comes, hold fast there,
Till what you do affect is ripn'd to ye.
Has the Duke seen ye yet?

HONORA
What if he have not?

ALINDA
You do your beauties too much wrong, appearing
So full of sweetness, newness; set so richly,
As if a Counsel beyond nature fram'd ye.

HONORA
If we were thus, say heaven had given these blessings,
Must we turn these to sin-oblations?

ALINDA
How foolishly this Countrey way shews in ye?
How full of flegm? do you come here to pray, Ladies?
You had best cry, stand away, let me alone Gentlemen,
I'le tell my Father else.

VIOLA
This woman's naught sure,
A very naughtie woman.

HONORA
Come, say on friend,
I'le be instructed by ye.

ALINDA
You'l thank me for't.

HONORA
Either I or the devil shall: The Duke you were speaking of.

ALINDA
'Tis well remembred: yes, let him first see you,
Appear not openly till he has view'd ye.

HONORA
He's a very noble Prince they say.

ALINDA
O wondrous gracious;
And as you may deliver your self at the first viewing.
For look ye, you must bear your self; yet take heed
It be so season'd with a sweet humilitie,
And grac'd with such a bountie in your beautie—

HONORA
But I hope he will offer me no ill?

ALINDA
No, no:
'Tis like he will kiss ye, and play with ye.

HONORA
Play with me, how?

ALINDA
Why, good Lord, that you are such a fool now!
No harm assure your self.

VIOLA
Will he play with me too?

ALINDA
Look babies in your eyes, my prettie sweet one:
There's a fine sport: do you know your lodgings yet?

HONORA
I hear of none.

ALINDA
I do then, they are handsom,
Convenient for access.

VIOLA
Access?

ALINDA
Yes little one,
For visitation of those friends and Servants,
Your beauties shall make choice of: friends and visits:
Do not you know those uses? Alas poor novice;
There's a close Cowch or two, handsomely placed too.

VIOLA
What are those I pray you?

ALINDA
Who would be troubled with such raw things? they are to lie upon,
And your love by ye; and discourse, and toy in.

VIOLA
Alas I have no love.

ALINDA
You must by any means:

You'l have a hundred, fear not.

VIOLA
Honestie keep me:
What shall I doe with all those?

ALINDA
You'l find uses:
Ye are ignorant yet, let time work; you must learn too,
To lie handsomly in your bed a mornings, neatly drest
In a most curious Wastcoat, to set ye off well,
Play with your Bracelets, sing: you must learn to rhime too,
And riddle neatly; studie the hardest language,
And 'tis no matter whether it be sense, or no,
So it go seemlie off. Be sure ye profit
In kissing, kissing sweetly: there lies a main point,
A key that opens to all practick pleasure;
I'le help ye to a friend of mine shall teach ye,
And suddenlie: your Country way is fulsome.

HONORA
Have ye schools for all these mysteries?

ALINDA
O yes,
And several hours prefix'd to studie in:
Ye may have Kalenders to know the good hour,
And when to take a jewel: for the ill too,
When to refuse, with observations on 'em;
Under what Sign 'tis best meeting in an Arbor,
And in what Bower, and hour it works; a thousand,
When in a Coach, when in a private lodging,
With all their vertues.

HONORA
Have ye studied these?
How beastly they become your youth? how bawdily?
A woman of your tenderness, a teacher,
Teacher of these lewd Arts? of your full beauty?
A man made up in lust would loath this in ye:
The rankest Leacher, hate such impudence.
They say the Devil can assume heavens brightness,
And so appear to tempt us: sure thou art no woman.

ALINDA
I joy to find ye thus.

HONORA

Thou hast no tenderness,
No reluctation in thy heart: 'tis mischief.

ALINDA
All's one for that; read these and then be satisfi'd,
A few more private rules I have gather'd for ye,
Read 'em, and well observe 'em: so I leave ye.

[Exit.

VIOLA
A wondrous wicked woman: shame go with thee.

HONORA
What new Pandoras box is this? I'le see it,
Though presently I tear it. Read Thine Viola,
'Tis in our own wills to believe and follow.

Worthy Honora, as you have begun
In vertues spotless school, so forward run:
Pursue that nobleness, and chaste desire
You ever had, burn in that holy fire;
And a white Martyr to fair memorie
Give up your name, unsoil'd of infamy.

How's this? Read yours out Sister: this amazes me.

VIOLA
Fear not thou yet unblasted Violet,
Nor let my wanton words a doubt beget,
Live in that peace and sweetness of thy bud,
Remember whose thou art, and grow still good.
Remember what thou art, and stand a storie
Fit for thy noble Sex, and thine own glorie.

HONORA
I know not what to think.

VIOLA
Sure a good woman,
An excellent woman, Sister.

HONORA
It confounds me;
Let 'em use all their arts, if these be their ends,
The Court I say breeds the best foes and friends.
Come, let's be honest wench, and doe our best service.

VIOLA
A most excellent woman, I will love her.

[Exeunt.

ACTUS QUARTUS

SCÆNA PRIMA

Enter **OLYMPIA** with a Casket and **ALINDA**.

ALINDA
Madam, the Duke has sent for the two Ladies.

OLYMPIA
I prethee go: I know thy thoughts are with him.
Go, go Alinda, do not mock me more.
I have found thy heart wench, do not wrong thy Mistris,
Thy too much loving Mistris: do not abuse her.

ALINDA
By your own fair hands I understand ye not.

OLYMPIA
By thy own fair eyes I understand thee too much,
Too far, and built a faith there thou hast ruin'd.
Goe, and enjoy thy wish, thy youth, thy pleasure,
Enjoy the greatness no doubt he has promised,
Enjoy the service of all eyes that see thee,
The glory thou hast aim'd at, and the triumph:
Only this last love I ask, forget thy Mistris.

ALINDA
Oh, who has wrong'd me? who has ruin'd me?
Poor wretched Girle, what poyson is flung on thee?
Excellent vertue, from whence flows this anger?

OLYMPIA
Go, ask my Brother, ask the faith thou gav'st me,
Ask all my favours to thee, ask my love,
Last, thy forgetfulness of good: then flye me,
For we must part Alinda.

ALINDA
You are weary of me;
I must confess, I was never worth your service,

Your bounteous favours less; but that my duty,
My ready will, and all I had to serve ye—
O Heaven thou know'st my honestie.

OLYMPIA
No more:
Take heed, heaven has a justice: take this ring with ye,
This doting spell you gave me: too well Alinda,
Thou knew'st the vertue in't; too well I feel it:
Nay keep that too, it may sometimes remember ye,
When you are willing to forget who gave it,
And to what vertuous end.

ALINDA
Must I goe from ye?
Of all the sorrows sorrow has—must I part with ye?
Part with my noble Mistris?

OLYMPIA
Or I with thee wench.

ALINDA
And part stain'd with opinion? Farewel Lady,
Happy and blessed Lady, goodness keep ye:
Thus your poor Servant full of grief turns from ye,
For ever full of grief, for ever from ye.
I have no being now, no friends, no Country,
I wander heaven knows whither, heaven knows how.
No life, now you are lost: only mine innocence,
That little left me of my self, goes with me,
That's all my bread and comfort. I confess Madam,
Truely confess, the Duke has often courted me.

OLYMPIA
And pour'd his Soul into thee, won thee.

ALINDA
Do you think so?
Well, time that told this tale, will tell my truth too,
And say ye had a faithfull, honest Servant:
The business of my life is now to pray for ye,
Pray for your vertuous loves; Pray for your children,
When Heaven shall make ye happy.

OLYMPIA
How she wounds me!
Either I am undone, or she must go: take these with ye,
Some toyes may doe ye service; and this mony;

And when ye want, I love ye not so poorly,
Not yet Alinda, that I would see ye perish.
Prethee be good, and let me hear: look on me,
I love those eyes yet dearly; I have kiss'd thee,
And now I'le doe't again: Farewel Alinda,
I am too full to speak more, and too wretched.

[Exit.

ALINDA
You have my faith,
And all the world my fortune.

[Exit.

SCÆNA SECUNDA

Enter **THEODORE**.

THEODORE
I would fain hear
What becomes of these two Wenches:
And if I can, I will doe 'em good.

[Enter **GENTLEMAN**, passing over the Stage.

Do you hear my honest friend?
He knows no such name:
What a world of business,
Which by interpretation are meer nothings,
These things have here! 'Mass now I think on't better,
I wish he be not sent for one of them
To some of these by-lodgings: me thought I saw
A kind of reference in his face to Bawderie.

[Enter **GENTLEMAN**, with a **GENTLEWOMAN**, passing over the Stage.

He has her, but 'tis none of them: hold fast thief:
An excellent touzing knave. Mistris
You are to suffer your penance some half hour hence now.
How far a fine Court Custard with Plums in it
Will prevail with one of these waiting Gentlewomen,
They are taken with these soluble things exceedingly;
This is some yeoman o'th' bottles now that has sent for her,
That she calls Father: now woe to this Ale incense.
By your leave Sir.

[Enter a **SERVANT**.

SERVANT
Well Sir; what's your pleasure with me?

THEODORE
You do not know the way to the maids lodgings?

SERVANT
Yes indeed do I Sir.

THEODORE
But you will not tell me?

SERVANT
No indeed will not I, because you doubt it.

[Exit.

[Enter **2ND SERVANT**.

THEODORE
These are fine gim-cracks: hey, here comes another,
A Flagon full of wine in's hand, I take it.
Well met my friend, is that wine?

2ND SERVANT
Yes indeed is it.

THEODORE
Faith I'le drink on't then.

2ND SERVANT
Ye may, because ye have sworn Sir.

THEODORE
'Tis very good, I'le drink a great deal now Sir.

2ND SERVANT
I cannot help it Sir.

THEODORE
I'le drink more yet.

2ND SERVANT
'Tis in your own hands.

THEODORE
There's your pot, I thank ye.
Pray let me drink again.

2ND SERVANT
Faith but ye shall not.
Now have I sworn I take it. Fare ye well Sir.

[Exit.

[Enter **LADY**.

THEODORE
This is the fin'st place to live in I e're enter'd.
Here comes a Gentlewoman, and alone; I'le to her.
Madam, my Lord my Master.

LADY
Who's your Lord Sir?

THEODORE
The Lord Boroskey, Lady.

LADY
Pray excuse me:
Here's something for your pains: within this hour Sir,
One of the choice young Ladies shall attend him:
Pray let it be in that Chamber juts out to the water;
'Tis private and convenient: doe my humble service
To my honourable good Lord, I beseech ye Sir;
If it please you to visit a poor Lady—
You carrie the 'haviour of a noble Gentleman.

THEODORE
I shall be bold.

LADY
'Tis a good aptness in ye.
I lye here in the Wood-yard, the blue lodgings Sir;
They call me merrily the Lady of the — Sir;
A little I know what belongs to a Gentleman,
And if it please you take the pains.

[Exit.

THEODORE
Dear Lady, take the pains?
Why a horse would not take the pains that thou requir'st now,

To cleave old crab-tree: one of the choice young Ladies?
I would I had let this Bawd goe, she has frighted me;
I am cruelly afraid of one of my Tribe now;
But if they will doe, the Devil cannot stop 'em.
Why should he have a young Lady? are women now
O'th' nature of Bottles, to be stopt with Corks?
O the thousand little furies that flye here now!
How now Captain?

[Enter **PUTSKIE**.

PUTSKIE
I come to seek you out Sir,
And all the Town I have travell'd.

THEODORE
What's the news man?

PUTSKIE
That that concerns us all, and very nearly:
The Duke this night holds a great feast at Court,
To which he bids for guests all his old Counsellors,
And all his favourites: your Father's sent for.

THEODORE
Why he is neither in council, nor in favour.

PUTSKIE
That's it: have an eye now, or never, and a quick one,
An eye that must not wink from good intelligence.
I heard a Bird sing, they mean him no good office.

[Enter **ANCIENT**.

THEODORE
Art sure he sups here?

PUTSKIE
Sure as 'tis day.

THEODORE
'Tis like then:
How now, where hast thou been Ancient?

ANCIENT
Measuring the City:
I have left my Brooms at gate here;
By this time the Porter has stole 'em to sweep out Rascals.

THEODORE
Brooms?

ANCIENT
I have been crying Brooms all the town over,
And such a Mart I have made, there's no tread near it.
O the young handsom wenches, how they twitter'd,
When they but saw me shake my ware, and sing too;
Come hither Master Broom-man I beseech ye:
Good Master Broom-man hither, cries another.

THEODORE
Thou art a mad fellow.

ANCIENT
They are all as mad as I: they all have trades now,
And roar about the streets like Bull-beggers.

THEODORE
What company of Souldiers are they?

ANCIENT
By this means I have gather'd
Above a thousand tall and hardy Souldiers,
If need be Colonel.

THEODORE
That need's come Ancient,
And 'twas discreetly done: goe, draw 'em presently,
But without suspicion: this night we shall need 'em;
Let 'em be near the Court, let Putskie guide 'em;
And wait me for occasion: here I'le stay still.

PUTSKIE
If it fall out we are ready; if not we are scatter'd:
I'le wait ye at an inch.

THEODORE
Doe, Farewel.

[Exeunt.

SCÆNA TERTIA

Enter **DUKE**, **BOROSKIE**.

DUKE
Are the Souldiers still so mutinous?

BOROSKIE
More than ever,
No Law nor Justice frights 'em: all the Town over
They play new pranks and gambols: no mans person,
Of what degree soever, free from abuses:
And durst they doe this, (let your grace consider)
These monstrous, most offensive things, these villanies,
If not set on, and fed? if not by one
They honour more than you? and more aw'd by him?

DUKE
Happily their own wants.

BOROSKIE
I offer to supply 'em,
And every hour make tender of their moneys:
They scorn it, laugh at me that offer it:
I fear the next device will be my life Sir;
And willingly I'le give it, so they stay there.

DUKE
Do you think Lord Archas privie?

BOROSKIE
More than thought,
I know it Sir, I know they durst not doe
These violent rude things, abuse the State thus,
But that they have a hope by his ambitions—

DUKE
No more: he's sent for?

BOROSKIE
Yes, and will be here sure.

DUKE
Let me talk further with you anon.

BOROSKIE
I'le wait Sir.

DUKE
Did you speak to the Ladies?

BOROSKIE
They'l attend your grace presently.

DUKE
How do you like 'em?

BOROSKIE
My eyes are too dull Judges.
They wait here Sir.

[Exit.

[Enter **HONORA** and **VIOLA**.

DUKE
Be you gone then: Come in Ladies,
Welcom to th' court sweet beauties; now the court shines,
When such true beams of beauty strike amongst us:
Welcom, welcom, even as your own joyes welcom.
How do you like the Court? how seems it to you?
Is't not a place created for all sweetness?
Why were you made such strangers to this happiness?
Barr'd the delights this holds? the richest jewels
Set ne're so well, if then not worn to wonder,
By judging eyes not set off, lose their lustre:
Your Country shades are faint; blasters of beauty;
The manners like the place, obscure and heavie;
The Rose buds of the beauties turn to cankers,
Eaten with inward thoughts: whilst there ye wander.
Here Ladies, here, you were not made for Cloisters,
Here is the Sphere you move in: here shine nobly,
And by your powerfull influence command all:
What a sweet modestie dwells round about 'em,
And like a nipping morn pulls in their blossoms?

HONORA
Your grace speaks cunningly, you doe not this,
I hope Sir, to betray us; we are poor triumphs;
Nor can our loss of honour adde to you Sir:
Great men, and great thoughts, seek things great and worthy,
Subjects to make 'em live, and not to lose 'em;
Conquests so nobly won, can never perish;
We are two simple maids, untutor'd here Sir;
Two honest maids, is that a sin at Court Sir?
Our breeding is obedience, but to good things,
To vertuous and to fair: what wou'd you win on us?
Why do I ask that question, when I have found ye?
Your Preamble has pour'd your heart out to us;

You would dishonour us; which in your translation
Here at the Court reads thus, your grace would love us,
Most dearly love us: stick us up for mistresses:
Most certain, there are thousands of our sex Sir
That would be glad of this, and handsom women,
And crowd into this favour, fair young women,
Excellent beauties Sir: when ye have enjoy'd 'em,
And suckt those sweets they have, what Saints are these then?
What worship have they won? what name you ghess Sir,
What storie added to their time, a sweet one?

DUKE
A brave spirited wench.

HONORA
I'le tell your grace,
And tell ye true: ye are deceiv'd in us two,
Extreamly cozen'd Sir: And yet in my eye
You are the handsomst man I ever lookt on,
The goodliest Gentleman; take that hope with ye;
And were I fit to be your wife (so much I honour ye)
Trust me I would scratch for ye but I would have ye.
I would wooe you then.

DUKE
She amazes me:
But how am I deceiv'd?

HONORA
O we are too honest,
Believe it Sir, too honest, far too honest,
The way that you propound too ignorant,
And there is no medling with us; for we are fools too,
Obstinate, peevish fools: if I would be ill,
And had a wantons itch, to kick my heels up,
I would not leap into th' Sun, and doe't there,
That all the world might see me: an obscure shade Sir,
Dark as the deed, there is no trusting light with it,
Nor that that's lighter far, vain-glorious greatness.

DUKE
You will love me as your friend?

HONORA
I will honour ye,
As your poor humble handmaid serve, and pray for ye.

DUKE

What sayes my little one; you are not so obstinate?
Lord how she blushes: here are truly fair souls:
Come you will be my love?

VIOLA
Good Sir be good to me,
Indeed I'le doe the best I can to please ye;
I do beseech your grace: Alas I fear ye.

DUKE
What shouldst thou fear?

HONORA
Fie Sir, this is not noble.

DUKE
Why do I stand entreating, where my power—

HONORA
You have no power, at least you ought to have none
In bad and beastly things: arm'd thus, I'le dye here,
Before she suffer wrong.

DUKE
Another Archas?

HONORA
His child Sir, and his spirit.

DUKE
I'le deal with you then,
For here's the honour to be won: sit down sweet,
Prethee Honora sit.

HONORA
Now ye intreat I will Sir.

DUKE
I doe, and will deserve it.

HONORA
That's too much kindness.

DUKE
Prethee look on me.

HONORA
Yes: I love to see ye,

And could look on an age thus, and admire ye:
Whilst ye are good and temperate I dare touch ye,
Kiss your white hand.

DUKE
Why not my lips?

HONORA
I dare Sir.

DUKE
I do not think ye dare.

HONORA
I am no coward.
Do you believe me now? or now? or now Sir?
You make me blush: but sure I mean no ill Sir:
It had been fitter you had kiss'd me.

DUKE
That I'le doe too.
What hast thou wrought into me?

HONORA
I hope all goodness:
Whilst ye are thus, thus honest, I dare do any thing,
Thus hang about your neck, and thus doat on ye;
Bless those fair lights: hell take me if I durst not—
But good Sir pardon me. Sister come hither,
Come hither, fear not wench: come hither, blush not,
Come kiss the Prince, the vertuous Prince, the good Prince:
Certain he is excellent honest.

DUKE
Thou wilt make me—

HONORA
Sit down, and hug him softly.

DUKE
Fie Honora,
Wanton Honora; is this the modesty,
The noble chastity your on-set shew'd me,
At first charge beaten back? Away.

HONORA
Thank ye:
Upon my knees I pray, heaven too may thank ye;

Ye have deceiv'd me cunningly, yet nobly
Ye have cozen'd me: In all your hopefull life yet,
A Scene of greater honour you ne're acted:
I knew fame was a lyar, too long, and loud tongu'd,
And now I have found it: O my vertuous Master.

VIOLA
My vertuous Master too.

HONORA
Now you are thus,
What shall become of me let fortune cast for't.

[Enter **ALINDA**.

DUKE
I'le be that fortune, if I live Honora,
Thou hast done a cure upon me, counsel could not.

ALINDA
Here take your ring Sir, and whom ye mean to ruine,
Give it to her next; I have paid for't dearly.

HONORA
A Ring to her?

DUKE
Why frowns my fair Alinda?
I have forgot both these again.

ALINDA
Stand still Sir,
Ye have that violent killing fire upon ye,
Consumes all honour, credit, faith.

HONORA
How's this?

ALINDA
My Royal Mistris favour towards me,
Woe-worth ye Sir, ye have poyson'd, blasted.

DUKE
I sweet?

ALINDA
You have taken that unmanly liberty,
Which in a worse man, is vain glorious feigning,

And kill'd my truth.

DUKE
Upon my life 'tis false wench.

ALINDA
Ladies,
Take heed, ye have a cunning gamester,
A handsom, and a high; come stor'd with Antidotes,
He has infections else will fire your blouds.

DUKE
Prethee Alinda hear me.

ALINDA
Words steept in hony,
That will so melt into your minds, buy Chastity,
A thousand wayes, a thousand knots to tie ye;
And when he has bound ye his, a thousand ruines.
A poor lost woman ye have made me.

DUKE
I'le maintain thee,
And nobly too.

ALINDA
That Gin's too weak to take me:
Take heed, take heed young Ladies: still take heed,
Take heed of promises, take heed of gifts,
Of forced feigned sorrows, sighs, take heed.

DUKE
By all that's mine, Alinda—

ALINDA
Swear
By your mischiefs:
O whither shall I goe?

DUKE
Go back again,
I'le force her take thee, love thee.

ALINDA
Fare ye well, Sir,
I will not curse ye; only this dwell with ye,
When ever ye love, a false belief light on ye.

[Exit.

HONORA
We'll take our leaves too, Sir.

DUKE
Part all the world now,
Since she is gone.

HONORA
You are crooked yet, dear Master,
And still I fear—

[Exeunt.

DUKE
I am vext,
And some shall find it.

[Exit.

SCÆNA QUARTA

Enter **ARCHAS** and a **SERVANT**.

ARCHAS
'Tis strange
To me to see the Court, and welcome:
O Royal place, how have I lov'd and serv'd thee?
Who lies on this side, know'st thou?

SERVANT
The Lord Burris.

ARCHAS
Thou hast nam'd a Gentleman
I stand much bound to:
I think he sent the Casket, Sir?

SERVANT
The same, Sir.

ARCHAS
An honest minded man, a noble Courtier:
The Duke made perfect choice when he took him.
Go you home, I shall hit the way

Without a guide now.

SERVANT
You may want something, Sir.

ARCHAS
Only my Horses,
Which after Supper let the Groom wait with:
I'le have no more attendance here.

SERVANT
Your will, Sir.

[Exit.

[Enter **THEODORE**.

THEODORE
You are well met here, Sir.

ARCHAS
How now boy,
How dost thou?

THEODORE
I should ask
You that question: how do you, Sir?
How do you feel your self?

ARCHAS
Why well, and lusty.

THEODORE
What do you here then?

ARCHAS
Why I am sent for
To Supper with the Duke.

THEODORE
Have you no meat at home?
Or do you long to feed as hunted Deer do,
In doubt and fear?

ARCHAS
I have an excellent stomach,
And can I use it better
Than among my friends, Boy?

How do the Wenches?

THEODORE
They do well enough, Sir,
They know the worst by this time: pray be rul'd, Sir,
Go home again, and if ye have a Supper,
Eat it in quiet there: this is no place for ye,
Especially at this time,
Take my word for't.

ARCHAS
May be they'll drink hard;
I could have drunk my share, Boy.
Though I am old, I will not out.

THEODORE
I hope you will.
Hark in your ear: the Court's
Too quick of hearing.

ARCHAS
Not mean me well?
Thou art abus'd and cozen'd.
Away, away.

THEODORE
To that end Sir, I tell ye.
Away, if you love your self.

ARCHAS
Who dare do these things,
That ever heard of honesty?

THEODORE
Old Gentleman,
Take a fools counsel.

ARCHAS
'Tis a fools indeed;
A very fools: thou hast more of
These flams in thee, these musty doubts:
Is't fit the Duke send for me,
And honour me to eat within his presence,
And I, like a tale fellow, play at bo-peep
With his pleasure?

THEODORE
Take heed

Of bo-peep with your pate, your pate, Sir,
I speak plain language now.

ARCHAS
If 'twere not here,
Where reverence bids me hold,
I would so swinge thee, thou rude,
Unmanner'd Knave; take from his bounty,
His honour that he gives me, to beget
Sawcy, and sullen fears?

THEODORE
You are not mad sure:
By this fair light, I speak
But what is whisper'd,
And whisper'd for a truth.

ARCHAS
A Dog: drunken people,
That in their Pot see visions,
And turn states, mad-men and Children:
Prethee do not follow me;
I tell thee I am angry:
Do not follow me.

THEODORE
I am as angry
As you for your heart,
I and as wilful too: go, like a Wood-cock,
And thrust your neck i'th' noose.

ARCHAS
I'le kill thee,
And thou speakst but three words more.
Do not follow me.

[Exit.

THEODORE
A strange old foolish fellow: I shall hear yet,
And if I do not my part, hiss at me.

[Exit.

SCÆNA QUINTA

Enter two **SERVANTS** preparing a Banquet.

1ST SERVANT
Believe me fellow here will be lusty drinking.
Many a washt pate in Wine I warrant thee.

2ND SERVANT
I am glad the old General's come: upon my Conscience
That joy will make half the Court drunk. Hark the Trumpets,
They are coming on; away.

1ST SERVANT
We'll have a rowse too.

[Exeunt.

Enter **DUKE, ARCHAS, BURRIS, BOROSKIE, ATTENDANTS, GENTLEMAN**.

DUKE
Come seat your selves: Lord Archas sit you there.

ARCHAS
'Tis far above my worth.

DUKE
I'le have it so:
Are all things ready?

BOROSKIE
All the Guards are set,
The Court Gates are shut.

DUKE
Then do as I prescrib'd ye.
Be sure no further.

BOROSKIE
I shall well observe ye.

DUKE
Come bring some wine: here's to my Sister, Gentlemen;
A health, and mirth to all.

ARCHAS
Pray fill it full, Sir.
'Tis a high health to vertue: here Lord Burris,
A maiden health: you are most fit to pledge it,
You have a maiden soul and much I honour it.

Passion o' me, ye are sad man.

DUKE
How now, Burris?
Go to, no more of this.

ARCHAS
Take the rowse freely,
'Twill warm your bloud, and make ye fit for jollity.
Your Graces pardon: when we get a cup, Sir,
We old men prate a pace.

DUKE
Mirth makes a Banquet;
As you love me no more.

BURRIS
I thank your Grace.
Give me it; Lord Boroskie.

BOROSKIE
I have ill brains, Sir.

BURRIS
Damnable ill, I know it.

BOROSKIE
But I'le pledge, Sir,
This vertuous health.

BURRIS
The more unfit for thy mouth.

[Enter two **SERVANTS** with Cloaks.

DUKE
Come, bring out Robes, and let my guests look nobly,
Fit for my love and presence: begin downward.
Off with your Cloaks, take new.

ARCHAS
Your grace deals truly,
Like a munificent Prince, with your poor subjects,
Who would not fight for you? what cold dull coward
Durst seek to save his life when you would ask it?
Begin a new health in your new adornments,
The Dukes, the Royal Dukes: ha! what have I got
Sir? ha! the Robe of death?

DUKE
You have deserv'd it.

ARCHAS
The Livery of the Grave? do you start all from me?
Do I smell of earth already? Sir, look on me,
And like a man; is this your entertainment?
Do you bid your worthiest guests to bloudy Banquets?

[Enter a **GUARD**.

A Guard upon me too? this is too foul play
Boy to thy good, thine honour: thou wretched Ruler,
Thou Son of fools and flatterers, Heir of hypocrites,
Am I serv'd in a Hearse that sav'd ye all?
Are ye men or Devils? Do ye gape upon me,
Wider, and swallow all my services?
Entomb them first, my faith next, then my integrity,
And let these struggle with your mangy minds,
Your sear'd, and seal'd up Consciences, till they burst.

BOROSKIE
These words are death.

ARCHAS
No those deeds that want rewards, Sirrah,
Those Battels I have fought, those horrid dangers,
Leaner than death, and wilder than destruction,
I have march'd upon, these honour'd wounds, times story,
The bloud I have lost, the youth, the sorrows suffer'd,
These are my death, these that can ne're be recompenced,
These that ye sit a brooding on like Toads,
Sucking from my deserts the sweets and favours,
And render me no pay again but poysons.

BOROSKIE
The proud vain Souldier thou hast set—

ARCHAS
Thou lyest.
Now by my little time of life lyest basely,
Malitiously and loudly: how I scorn thee!
If I had swel'd the Souldier, or intended
An act in person, leaning to dishonour,
As ye would fain have forced me, witness Heaven,
Where clearest understanding of all truth is,
(For these are spightful men, and know no piety)

When Olin came, grim Olin, when his marches,
His last Incursions made the City sweat,
And drove before him, as a storm drives Hail,
Such showrs of frosted fears, shook all your heart-strings;
Then when the Volga trembled at his terrour,
And hid his seven curl'd heads, afraid of bruising,
By his arm'd Horses hoofs; had I been false then,
Or blown a treacherous fire into the Souldier,
Had but one spark of villany liv'd within me,
Ye'ad had some shadow for this black about me.
Where was your Souldiership? why went not you out?
And all your right honourable valour with ye?
Why met ye not the Tartar, and defi'd him?
Drew your dead-doing sword, and buckl'd with him?
Shot through his Squadrons like a fiery Meteor?
And as we see a dreadful clap of Thunder
Rend the stiffhearted Oaks, and toss their roots up:
Why did not you so charge him? you were sick then,
You that dare taint my credit slipt to bed then,
Stewing and fainting with the fears ye had,
A whorson shaking fit opprest your Lordship:
Blush Coward, Knave, and all the world hiss at thee.

DUKE
Exceed not my command.

[Exit.

BOROSKIE
I shall observe it.

ARCHAS
Are you gone too? Come weep not honest Burris,
Good loving Lord, no more tears: 'tis not his malice,
This fellows malice, nor the Dukes displeasure,
By bold bad men crowded into his nature,
Can startle me: fortune ne're raz'd this Fort yet:
I am the same, the same man, living, dying;
The same mind to 'em both, I poize thus equal;
Only the jugling way that toll'd me to it,
The Judas way, to kiss me, bid me welcome,
And cut my throat, a little sticks upon me.
Farewel, commend me to his Grace, and tell him,
The world is full of servants, he may have many:
And some I wish him honest: he's undone else:
But such another doating Archas never,
So try'd and touch'd a faith: farewell for ever.

BURRIS
Be strong my Lord: you must not go thus lightly.

ARCHAS
Now, what's to do? what sayes the Law unto me?
Give me my great offence that speaks me guilty.

BOROSKIE
Laying aside a thousand petty matters,
As scorns, and insolencies both from your self and followers,
Which you put first fire to, and these are deadly,
I come to one main cause, which though it carries
A strangeness in the circumstance, it carries death too,
Not to be pardon'd neither: ye have done a sacriledge.

ARCHAS
High Heaven defend me man: how, how Boroskie?

BOROSKIE
Ye have took from the Temple those vow'd Arms,
The holy Ornament you hung up there,
No absolution of your vow, no order
From holy Church to give 'em back unto you
After they were purified from War, and rested
From bloud, made clean by ceremony: from the Altar
You snatch'd 'em up again, again ye wore 'em,
Again you stain'd 'em, stain'd your vow, the Church too,
And rob'd it of that right was none of yours, Sir,
For which the Law requires your head, ye know it.

ARCHAS
Those arms I fought in last?

BOROSKIE
The same.

ARCHAS
God a mercy,
Thou hast hunted out a notable cause to kill me:
A subtle one: I dye, for saving all you;
Good Sir, remember if you can, the necessity,
The suddenness of time, the state all stood in;
I was entreated to, kneel'd to, and pray'd to,
The Duke himself, the Princes, all the Nobles,
The cries of Infants, Bed-rid Fathers, Virgins;
Prethee find out a better cause, a handsomer,
This will undo thee too: people will spit at thee,
The Devil himself would be asham'd of this cause;

Because my haste made me forget the ceremony,
The present danger every where, must my life satisfie?

BOROSKIE
It must, and shall.

ARCHAS
 O base ungrateful people,
Have ye no other Swords to cut my throat with
But mine own nobleness? I confess, I took 'em,
The vow not yet absolv'd I hung 'em up with:
Wore 'em, fought in 'em, gilded 'em again
In the fierce Tartars blouds; for you I took 'em,
For your peculiar safety, Lord, for all,
I wore 'em for my Countries health, that groan'd then:
Took from the Temple, to preserve the Temple;
That holy place, and all the sacred monuments,
The reverent shrines of Saints, ador'd and honour'd,
Had been consum'd to ashes, their own sacrifice;
Had I been slack, or staid that absolution,
No Priest had liv'd to give it; my own honour,
Cure of my Country murder me?

BOROSKIE
No, no Sir,
I shall force that from ye, will make this cause light too,
Away with him: I shall pluck down that heart, Sir.

ARCHAS
Break it thou mayest; but if it bend, for pity,
Doggs, and Kites eat it: come I am honours Martyr.

[Exit.

SCÆNA SEXTA

Enter **DUKE** and **BURRIS**.

DUKE
Exceed my Warrant?

BURRIS
You know he loves him not.

DUKE
He dares as well eat death, as do it, eat wild-fire,

Through a few fears I mean to try his goodness,
That I may find him fit, to wear here, Burris;
I know Boroskie hates him, to death hates him,
I know he's a Serpent too, a swoln one,

[Noise within.

But I have pull'd his sting out: what noise is that?

THEODORE
within. Down with 'em, down with 'em, down with the gates.

SOULDIER [within]
Stand, stand, stand.

PUTSKIE
within. Fire the Palace before ye.

BURRIS
Upon my life the Souldier, Sir, the Souldier,
A miserable time is come.

[Enter **GENTLEMAN**.

GENTLEMAN
Oh save him,
Upon my knees, my hearts knees, save Lord Archas,
We are undone else.

DUKE
Dares he touch his Body?

GENTLEMAN
He racks him fearfully, most fearfully.

DUKE
Away Burris,
Take men, and take him from him; clap him up,
And if I live, I'll find a strange death for him.

[Exit **BURRIS**.

Are the Souldiers broke in?

GENTLEMAN
By this time sure they are, Sir,
They beat the Gates extreamly, beat the people.

DUKE
Get me a guard about me; make sure the lodgings,
And speak the Souldiers fair.

GENTLEMAN
Pray Heaven that take, Sir.

[Exeunt.

[Enter **PUTSKIE**, **ANCIENT**, **SOULDIERS** with Torches.

PUTSKIE
Give us the General, we'll fire the Court else,
Render him safe and well.

ANCIENT
Do not fire the Cellar,
There's excellent Wine in't, Captain, and though it be cold weather,
I do not love it mull'd; bring out the General,
We'll light ye such a Bone-fire else: where are ye?
Speak, or we'll toss your Turrets, peep out of your Hives,
We'll smoak ye else: Is not that a Nose there?
Put out that Nose again, and if thou dar'st
But blow it before us: now he creeps out on's Burrough.

[Enter **GENTLEMAN**.

PUTSKIE
Give us the General.

GENTLEMAN
Yes, Gentlemen;
Or any thing ye can desire.

ANCIENT
You musk-cat,
Cordevant-skin we will not take your answer.

PUTSKIE
Where is the Duke? speak suddenly, and send him hither.

ANCIENT
Or we'll so frye your Buttocks.

GENTLEMAN
Good sweet Gentlemen—

ANCIENT

We are neither good nor sweet, we are Souldiers,
And you miscreants that abuse the General.
Give fire my Boys, 'tis a dark Evening,
Let's light 'em to their lodgings.

[Enter **OLYMPIA**, **HONORA**, **VIOLA**, **THEODORE**, **WOMEN**.

HONORA
Good Brother be not fierce.

THEODORE
I will not hurt her,
Fear not sweet Lady.

OLYMPIA
Nay, do what you please, Sir,
I have a sorrow that exceeds all yours,
And more, contemns all danger.

[Enter **DUKE**, above.

THEODORE
Where is the Duke?

DUKE
He's here; what would ye Souldiers? wherefore troop ye
Like mutinous mad-men thus?

THEODORE
Give me my Father.

PUTSKIE and ANCIENT
Give us our General.

THEODORE
Set him here before us,
Ye see the pledge we have got; ye see the Torches;
All shall to ashes, as I live, immediately,
A thousand lives for one.

DUKE
But hear me?

PUTSKIE
No, we come not to dispute.

[Enter **ARCHAS** and **BURRIS**.

THEODORE
By Heaven I swear he's rackt and whipt.

HONORA
Oh my poor Father!

PUTSKIE
Burn, kill and burn.

ARCHAS
Hold, hold, I say: hold Souldiers,
On your allegiance hold.

THEODORE
We must not.

ARCHAS
Hold:
I swear by Heaven he is a barbarous Traitor stirs first,
A Villain, and a stranger to Obedience,
Never my Souldier more, nor Friend to Honour:
Why did you use your old Man thus? thus cruelly
Torture his poor weak Body? I ever lov'd ye.

DUKE
Forget me in these wrongs, most noble Archas.

ARCHAS
I have balm enough for all my hurts: weep no more Sir
A satisfaction for a thousand sorrows;
I do believe you innocent, a good man,
And Heaven forgive that naughty thing that wrong'd me:
Why look ye wild, my friends? why stare ye on me?
I charge ye, as ye are men, my men, my lovers,
As ye are honest faithful men, fair Souldiers,
Let down your anger: Is not this our Soveraign?
The head of mercy, and of Law? who dares then,
But Rebels, scorning Law, appear thus violent?
Is this a place for Swords? for threatning fires?
The Reverence of this House dares any touch,
But with obedient knees, and pious duties?
Are we not all his Subjects? all sworn to him?
Has not he power to punish our offences?
And do we not daily fall into 'em? assure your selves
I did offend, and highly, grievously,
This good, sweet Prince I offended, my life forfeited,
Which yet his mercy and his old love met with,
And only let me feel his light rod this way:

Ye are to thank him for your General,
Pray for his life and fortune; swear your bloods for him.
Ye are offenders too, daily offenders,
Proud insolencies dwell in your hearts, and ye do 'em,
Do 'em against his Peace, his Law, his Person;
Ye see he only sorrows for your sins,
And where his power might persecute, forgives ye:
For shame put up your Swords, for honesty,
For orders sake, and whose ye are, my Souldiers,
Be not so rude.

THEODORE
They have drawn blood from you, Sir.

ARCHAS
That was the blood rebell'd, the naughty blood,
The proud provoking blood; 'tis well 'tis out, Boy;
Give you example first; draw out, and orderly.

HONORA
Good Brother, do.

ARCHAS
Honest and high example,
As thou wilt have my Blessing follow thee,
Inherit all mine honours: thank ye Theodore,
My worthy Son.

THEODORE
If harm come, thank your self, Sir,
I must obey ye.

[Exit.

ARCHAS
Captain, you know the way now:
A good man, and a valiant, you were ever,
Inclin'd to honest things; I thank ye, Captain.

[Exit **SOULDIERS**.

Souldiers, I thank ye all: and love me still,
But do not love me so you lose Allegiance,
Love that above your lives: once more I thank ye.

DUKE
Bring him to rest, and let our cares wait on him;
Thou excellent old man, thou top of honour,

Where Justice, and Obedience only build,
Thou stock of Vertue, how am I bound to love thee!
In all thy noble ways to follow thee!

BURRIS
Remember him that vext him, Sir.

DUKE
Remember?
When I forget that Villain, and to pay him
For all his mischiefs, may all good thoughts forget me.

ARCHAS
I am very sore.

DUKE
Bring him to Bed with ease, Gentlemen,
For every stripe I'll drop a tear to wash 'em,
And in my sad Repentance—

ARCHAS
'Tis too much,
I have a life yet left to gain that love, Sir.

[Exeunt.

ACTUS QUINTUS

SCÆNA PRIMA

Enter **DUKE**, **BURRIS** and **GENTLEMEN**.

DUKE
How does Lord Archas?

BURRIS
But weak, and't please ye;
Yet all the helps that art can, are applied to him;
His heart's untoucht, and whole yet; and no doubt, Sir,
His mind being sound, his body soon will follow.

DUKE
O that base Knave that wrong'd him, without leave too;
But I shall find an hour to give him thanks for't;
He's fast, I hope.

BURRIS
As fast as irons can keep him:
But the most fearful Wretch—

DUKE
He has a Conscience,
A cruel stinging one I warrant him,
A loaden one: But what news of the Souldier?
I did not like their parting, 'twas too sullen.

BURRIS
That they keep still, and I fear a worse clap;
They are drawn out of the Town, and stand in counsels,
Hatching unquiet thoughts, and cruel purposes:
I went my self unto 'em, talkt with the Captains,
Whom I found fraught with nothing but loud murmurs,
And desperate curses, sounding these words often
Like Trumpets to their angers: we are ruin'd,
Our services turn'd to disgraces, mischiefs;
Our brave old General, like one had pilfer'd,
Tortur'd, and whipt: the Colonels eyes, like torches,
Blaze every where and fright fair peace.

GENTLEMAN
Yet worse, Sir;
The news is currant now, they mean to leave ye,
Leave their Allegiance; and under Olins Charge
The bloody Enemy march straight against ye.

BURRIS
I have heard this too, Sir.

DUKE
This must be prevented,
And suddenly, and warily.

BURRIS
'Tis time, Sir,
But what to minister, or how?

DUKE
Go in with me,
And there we'll think upon't: such blows as these,
Equal defences ask, else they displease.

[Exeunt.

SCÆNA SECUNDA

Enter **PETESCA** and **GENTLEWOMEN**.

PETESCA
Lord, what a coil has here been with these Souldiers!
They are cruel fellows.

WOMAN
And yet methought we found 'em
Handsome enough; I'll tell thee true, Petesca,
I lookt for other manner of dealings from 'em,
And had prepar'd my self; but where's my Lady?

PETESCA
In her old dumps within: monstrous melancholy;
Sure she was mad of this Wench.

WOMAN
And she had been a man,
She would have been a great deal madder, I am glad she is shifted.

PETESCA
'Twas a wicked thing for me to betray her,
And yet I must confess she stood in our lights.

[Enter **ALINDA**.

What young thing's this?

ALINDA
Good morrow beauteous Gentlewomen:
'Pray ye is the Princess stirring yet?

WOMAN
He has her face.

PETESCA
Her very tongue, and tone too: her youth upon him.

ALINDA
I guess ye to be the Princess Women.

PETESCA
Yes, we are, Sir.

ALINDA

Pray is there not a Gentlewoman waiting on her Grace,
Ye call Alinda?

PETESCA
The Devil sure in her shape.

WOMAN
I have heard her tell my Lady of a Brother,
An only Brother that she had: in travel—

PETESCA
'Mass, I remember that: this may be he too:
I would this thing would serve her.

[Enter **OLYMPIA**.

WOMAN
So would I Wench,
We should love him better sure: Sir, here's the Princess,
She best can satisfie ye.

ALINDA
How I love that presence!
O blessed Eyes, how nobly shine your comforts!

OLYMPIA
What Gentleman is that?

WOMAN
We know not, Madam:
He ask'd us for your Grace: and as we guess it,
He is Alinda's Brother.

OLYMPIA
Ha! let me mark him:
My grief has almost blinded me: her Brother?
By Venus, he has all her sweetness upon him:
Two silver drops of dew were never liker.

ALINDA
Gracious Lady—

OLYMPIA
That pleasant pipe he has too.

ALINDA
Being my happiness to pass by this way,
And having as I understand by Letters,

A Sister in your vertuous service, Madam—

OLYMPIA
O now my heart, my heart akes.

ALINDA
All the comfort
My poor youth has, all that my hopes have built me,
I thought it my first duty, my best service,
Here to arrive first, humbly to thank your Grace
For my poor Sister, humbly to thank your Nobleness,
That bounteous Goodness in ye.

OLYMPIA
'Tis he certainly.

ALINDA
That spring of favour to her; with my life, Madam,
If any such most happy means might meet me,
To shew my thankfulness.

OLYMPIA
What have I done, Fool!

ALINDA
She came a stranger to your Grace, no Courtier;
Nor of that curious breed befits your service,
Yet one I dare assure my Soul, that lov'd ye
Before she saw ye; doted on your Vertues;
Before she knew those fair eyes, long'd to read 'em,
You only had her prayers, you her wishes;
And that one hope to be yours once, preserv'd her.

OLYMPIA
I have done wickedly.

ALINDA
A little Beauty,
Such as a Cottage breeds, she brought along with her;
And yet our Country-eyes esteem'd it much too:
But for her beauteous mind, forget great Lady,
I am her Brother, and let me speak a stranger,
Since she was able to beget a thought, 'twas honest.
The daily study how to fit your services,
Truly to tread that vertuous path you walk in,
So fir'd her honest Soul, we thought her Sainted;
I presume she is still the same: I would fain see her,
For Madam, 'tis no little love I owe her.

OLYMPIA
Sir, such a maid there was, I had—

ALINDA
There was, Madam?

OLYMPIA
O my poor Wench: eyes, I will ever curse ye
For your Credulity, Alinda.

ALINDA
That's her name, Madam.

OLYMPIA
Give me a little leave, Sir, to lament her.

ALINDA
Is she dead, Lady?

OLYMPIA
Dead, Sir, to my service.
She is gone, pray ye ask no further.

ALINDA
I obey Madam:
Gone? now must I lament too: said ye gone Madam?

OLYMPIA
Gone, gone for ever.

ALINDA
That's a cruel saying:
Her honour too?

OLYMPIA
Prithee look angry on me,
And if thou ever lovedst her, spit upon me;
Do something like a Brother, like a friend,
And do not only say thou lov'st her—

ALINDA
Ye amaze me.

OLYMPIA
I ruin'd her, I wrong'd her, I abus'd her;
Poor innocent soul, I flung her; sweet Alinda,
Thou vertuous maid, my soul now calls thee vertuous.

Why do ye not rail now at me?

ALINDA
For what Lady?

OLYMPIA
Call me base treacherous woman.

ALINDA
Heaven defend me.

OLYMPIA
Rashly I thought her false, and put her from me,
Rashly, and madly I betrai'd her modesty,
Put her to wander, heaven knows where: nay, more Sir,
Stuck a black brand upon her.

ALINDA
'Twas not well Lady.

OLYMPIA
'Twas damnable: she loving me so dearly,
Never poor wench lov'd so: Sir believe me,
'Twas the most dutious wench, the best companion,
When I was pleas'd, the happiest, and the gladdest,
The modestest sweet nature dwelt within her:
I saw all this, I knew all this, I lov'd it,
I doated on it too, and yet I kill'd it:
O what have I forsaken? what have I lost?

ALINDA
Madam, I'le take my leave, since she is wandring,
'Tis fit I know no rest.

OLYMPIA
Will you go too Sir?
I have not wrong'd you yet, if you dare trust me,
For yet I love Alinda there, I honour her,
I love to look upon those eyes that speak her,
To read that face again, (modesty keep me,)
Alinda, in that shape: but why should you trust me,
'Twas I betray'd your Sister, I undid her;
And believe me, gentle youth, 'tis I weep for her:
Appoint what penance you please: but stay then,
And see me perform it: ask what honour this place
Is able to heap on ye, or what wealth:
If following me will like ye, my care of ye,
Which for your sisters sake, for your own goodness—

ALINDA
Not all the honour earth has, now she's gone Lady,
Not all the favour; yet if I sought preferment,
Under your bounteous Grace I would only take it.
Peace rest upon ye: one sad tear every day
For poor Alindas. sake, 'tis fit ye pay.

[Exit.

OLYMPIA
A thousand noble youth, and when I sleep,
Even in my silver slumbers still I'le weep.

[Exit.

SCÆNA TERTIA

Enter **DUKE** and **GENTLEMAN**.

DUKE
Have ye been with 'em?

GENTLEMAN
Yes, and't please your Grace,
But no perswasion serves 'em, nor no promise,
They are fearfull angry, and by this time Sir,
Upon their march to the Enemy.

DUKE
They must be stopt.

[Enter **BURRIS**.

GENTLEMAN
I, but what force is able? and what leader—

DUKE
How now, have you been with Archas?

BURRIS
Yes, and't please ye,
And told him all: he frets like a chaf'd Lyon,
And calls for his Arms: and all those honest Courtiers
That dare draw Swords.

DUKE
Is he able to do any thing?

BURRIS
His mind is well enough; and where his charge is,
Let him be ne're so sore, 'tis a full Army.

DUKE
Who commands the Rebels?

BURRIS
The young Colonel,
That makes the old man almost mad: he swears Sir,
He will not spare his Sons head for the Dukedom.

DUKE
Is the Court in Arms?

BURRIS
As fast as they can bustle,
Every man mad to goe now: inspir'd strangely,
As if they were to force the Enemy,
I beseech your Grace to give me leave.

DUKE
Pray go Sir,
And look to the old man well; take up all fairly,
And let no bloud be spilt; take general pardons,
And quench this fury with fair peace.

BURRIS
I shall Sir,
Or seal it with my service; they are villains:
The Court is up: good Sir, go strengthen 'em,
Your Royal sight will make 'em scorn all dangers;
The General needs no proof.

DUKE
Come let's go view 'em.

[Exeunt.

SCÆNA QUARTA

Enter **THEODORE, PUTSKIE, ANCIENT, SOULDIERS**, Drums, and Colours.

THEODORE
'Tis known we are up, and marching: no submission,
No promise of base peace can cure our maladies,
We have suffer'd beyond all repair of honour:
Your valiant old man's whipt; whipt Gentlemen,
Whipt like a slave: that flesh that never trembled,
Nor shrunk one sinew at a thousand charges,
That noble body rib'd in arms, the Enemy
So often shook at, and then shun'd like thunder,
That body's torn with lashes.

ANCIENT
Let's turn head.

PUTSKIE
Turn nothing Gentlemen, let's march on fairly,
Unless they charge us.

THEODORE
Think still of his abuses,
And keep your angers.

ANCIENT
He was whipt like a top,
I never saw a whore so lac'd: Court school-butter?
Is this their diet? I'le dress 'em one running banquet:
What Oracle can alter us? did not we see him?
See him we lov'd?

THEODORE
And though we did obey him,
Forc'd by his reverence for that time; is't fit Gentlemen?
My noble friends, is't fit we men, and Souldiers,
Live to endure this, and look on too?

PUTSKIE
Forward:
They may call back the Sun as soon, stay time,
Prescribe a Law to death, as we endure this.

THEODORE
They will make ye all fair promises.

ANCIENT
We care not.

THEODORE
Use all their arts upon ye.

ANCIENT
Hang all their arts.

PUTSKIE
And happily they'l bring him with 'em.

ANCIENT
March apace then,
He is old and cannot overtake us.

PUTSKIE
Say he doe.

ANCIENT
We'l run away with him: they shall never see him more:
The truth is, we'l hear nothing, stop at nothing,
Consider nothing but our way; believe nothing,
Not though they say their prayers: be content with nothing,
But the knocking out their brains: and last, do nothing
But ban 'em and curse 'em, till we come to kill 'em.

THEODORE
Remove then forwards bravely; keep your minds whole,
And the next time we face 'em, shall be fatal.

[Exeunt.

SCÆNA QUINTA

Enter **ARCHAS**, **DUKE**, **BURRIS**, **GENTLEMAN** and **SOULDIERS**.

ARCHAS
Peace to your Grace; take rest Sir, they are before us.

GENTLEMAN
They are Sir, and upon the march.

[Exit **DUKE**.

ARCHAS
Lord Burris,
Take you those horse and coast 'em: upon the first advantage,
If they will not slake their march, charge 'em up roundly,
By that time I'le come in.

BURRIS
I'le do it truly.

[Exit.

GENTLEMAN
How do you feel your self Sir?

ARCHAS
Well, I thank ye;
A little weak, but anger shall supply that;
You will all stand bravely to it?

ALL
Whilst we have lives Sir.

ARCHAS
Ye speak like Gentlemen; I'le make the knaves know,
The proudest, and the strongest hearted Rebel,
They have a law to live in, and they shall have;
Beat up a pace, by this time he is upon 'em,

[Drum within.

And sword, but hold me now, thou shalt play ever.

[Exeunt.

[Enter Drums beating, **THEODORE**, **PUTSKIE**, **ANCIENT** and their **SOULDIERS**.

THEODORE
Stand, stand, stand close, and sure;

[Enter **BURRIS**, and 1 or 2 **SOULDIERS**.

The horse will charge us.

ANCIENT
Let 'em come on, we have provender fit for 'em.

PUTSKIE
Here comes Lord Burris Sir, I think to parly.

THEODORE
You are welcom noble Sir, I hope to our part.

BURRIS
No, valiant Colonel, I am come to chide ye,

To pity ye; to kill ye, if these fail me;
Fie, what dishonour seek ye! what black infamy!
Why do ye draw out thus? draw all shame with ye?
Are these fit cares in subjects? I command ye
Lay down your arms again, move in that peace,
That fair obedience you were bred in.

PUTSKIE
Charge us:
We come not here to argue.

THEODORE
Charge up bravely,
And hotly too, we have hot spleens to meet ye,
Hot as the shames are offer'd us.

[Enter **ARCHAS**, **GENTLEMAN** and **SOULDIERS**.

BURRIS
Look behind ye.
Do you see that old man? do you know him Souldiers?

PUTSKIE
Your Father Sir, believe me—

BURRIS
You know his marches,
You have seen his executions: is it yet peace?

THEODORE
We'l dye here first.

BURRIS
Farewel: you'l hear on's presently.

ARCHAS
Stay Burris: this is too poor, too beggerly a body
To bear the honour of a charge from me,
A sort of tatter'd Rebels; go provide Gallowses;
Ye are troubled with hot heads, I'le cool ye presently:
These look like men that were my Souldiers
Now I behold 'em nearly, and more narrowly,
My honest friends: where got they these fair figures?
Where did they steal these shapes?

BURRIS
They are struck already.

ARCHAS
Do you see that fellow there, that goodly Rebel?
He looks as like a Captain I lov'd tenderly:
A fellow of a faith indeed.

BURRIS
He has sham'd him.

ARCHAS
And that that bears the Colours there, most certain
So like an Ancient of mine own, a brave fellow,
A loving and obedient, that believe me Burris,
I am amaz'd and troubled: and were it not
I know the general goodness of my people,
The duty, and the truth, the stedfast honestie,
And am assur'd they would as soon turn Devils
As rebels to allegeance, for mine honour.

BURRIS
Here needs no wars.

PUTSKIE
I pray forgive us Sir.

ANCIENT
Good General forgive us, or use your sword,
Your words are double death.

ALL
Good noble General.

BURRIS
Pray Sir be mercifull.

ARCHAS
Weep out your shames first,
Ye make me fool for companie: fie Souldiers,
My Souldiers too, and play these tricks? what's he there?
Sure I have seen his face too; yes, most certain
I have a son, but I hope he is not here now,
'Would much resemble this man, wondrous near him,
Just of his height and making too, you seem a Leader.

THEODORE
Good Sir, do not shame me more: I know your anger,
And less than death I look not for.

ARCHAS

You shall be my charge Sir, it seems you want foes,
When you would make your friends your Enemies.
A running bloud ye have, but I shall cure ye.

BURRIS
Good Sir—

ANCIENT
No more good Lord: beat forward Souldiers:
And you, march in the rear, you have lost your places.

[Exeunt.

SCÆNA SEXTA

Enter **DUKE, OLYMPIA, HONORA, VIOLA**.

DUKE
You shall not be thus sullen still with me Sister,
You do the most unnobly to be angry,
For as I have a soul, I never touch'd her,
I never yet knew one unchast thought in her:
I must confess, I lov'd her: as who would not?
I must confess I doated on her strangely,
I offer'd all, yet so strong was her honour,
So fortifi'd as fair, no hope could reach her,
And whilst the world beheld this, and confirm'd it,
Why would you be so jealous?

OLYMPIA
Good Sir pardon me,
I feel sufficiently my follies penance,
And am asham'd, that shame a thousand sorrows
Feed on continually, would I had never seen her,
Or with a clearer judgement look'd upon her,
She was too good for me, so heavenly good Sir,
Nothing but Heaven can love that soul sufficiently,
Where I shall see her once again.

[Enter **BURRIS**.

DUKE
No more tears,
If she be within the Dukedom, we'l recover her:
Welcom Lord Burris, fair news I hope.

BURRIS
Most fair Sir,
Without one drop of bloud these wars are ended,
The Souldier cool'd again, indeed asham'd Sir,
And all his anger ended.

DUKE
Where's Lord Archas?

BURRIS
Not far off Sir: with him his valiant son,
Head of this fire, but now a prisoner,
And if by your sweet mercy not prevented,
I fear some fatal stroke.

[Drums.

[Enter **ARCHAS**, **THEODORE**, **GENTLEMEN**, **SOULDIERS**.

DUKE
I hear the Drums beat,
Welcom, my worthy friend.

ARCHAS
Stand where ye are Sir,
Even as you love your country, move not forward,
Nor plead for peace till I have done a justice,
A justice on this villain; none of mine now,
A justice on this Rebel.

HONORA
O my Brother.

ARCHAS
This fatal firebrand—

DUKE
Forget not old man,
He is thy son, of thine own bloud.

ARCHAS
In these veins
No treacherie e're harbour'd yet, no mutinie,
I ne're gave life to lewd and headstrong Rebels.

DUKE
'Tis his first fault.

ARCHAS
Not of a thousand Sir,
Or were it so, it is a fault so mightie,
So strong against the nature of all mercy,
His Mother were she living, would not weep for him,
He dare not say he would live.

THEODORE
I must not Sir,
Whilst you say 'tis not fit: your Graces mercy
Not to my life appli'd, but to my fault Sir,
The worlds forgiveness next, last, on my knees Sir,
I humbly beg,
Do not take from me yet the name of Father,
Strike me a thousand blows, but let me dye yours.

ARCHAS
He moves my heart: I must be suddain with him,
I shall grow faint else in my execution;
Come, come Sir, you have seen death; now meet him bravely.

DUKE
Hold, hold I say, a little hold, consider
Thou hast no more sons Archas to inherit thee.

ARCHAS
Yes Sir, I have another, and a nobler:
No treason shall inherit me: young Archas
A boy, as sweet as young, my Brother breeds him,
My noble Brother Briskie breeds him nobly,
Him let your favour find: give him your honour.

[Enter **PUTSKIE** (alias Briskie) and **ALINDA**, (alias Archas.)

PUTSKIE
Thou hast no child left Archas, none to inherit thee
If thou strikst that stroke now: behold young Archas;
Behold thy Brother here, thou bloudy Brother,
As bloody to this sacrifice as thou art:
Heave up thy sword, and mine's heav'd up: strike Archas,
And I'le strike too as suddenly, as deadly:
Have mercy, and I'le have mercy: the Duke gives it.
Look upon all these, how they weep it from thee,
Choose quickly, and begin.

DUKE
On your obedience,
On your allegeance save him.

ARCHAS
Take him to ye,

[**SOULDIERS** shout.

And sirrah, be an honest man, ye have reason:
I thank ye worthy Brother: welcom child,
Mine own sweet child.

DUKE
Why was this boy conceal'd thus?

PUTSKIE
Your graces pardon:
Fearing the vow you made against my Brother,
And that your anger would not only light
On him, but find out all his familie,
This young boy, to preserve from after danger,
Like a young wench, hither I brought; my self
In the habit of an ordinarie Captain
Disguis'd, got entertainment, and serv'd here
That I might still be ready to all fortunes:
That boy your Grace took, nobly entertain'd him,
But thought a Girle, Alinda, Madam.

OLYMPIA
Stand away,
And let me look upon him.

DUKE
My young Mistris?
This is a strange metamorphosis, Alinda?

ALINDA
Your graces humble servant.

DUKE
Come hither Sister:
I dare yet scarce believe mine eyes: how they view one another?
Dost thou not love this boy well?

OLYMPIA
I should lye else,
Trust me, extreamly lye Sir.

DUKE
Didst thou never wish Olympia,

It might be thus?

OLYMPIA
A thousand times.

DUKE
Here take him:
Nay, do not blush: I do not jest; kiss sweetly:
Boy, ye kiss faintly boy; Heaven give ye comfort;
Teach him, he'l quickly learn: there's two hearts eas'd now.

ARCHAS
You do me too much honour Sir.

DUKE
No Archas,
But all I can, I will; can you love me? speak truly.

HONORA
Yes Sir, dearly.

DUKE
Come hither Viola, can you love this man?

VIOLA
I'le do the best I can Sir.

DUKE
Seal it Burris,
We'l all to Church together instantly:
And then a vie for boyes; stay, bring Boroskie.

[Enter **BOROSKIE**.

I had almost forgot that lump of mischief.
There Archas, take the enemie to honour,
The knave to worth: do with him what thou wilt.

ARCHAS
Then to my sword again; you to your prayers;
Wash off your villanies, you feel the burthen.

BOROSKIE
Forgive me e're I die, most honest Archas;
'Tis too much honour that I perish thus;
O strike my faults to kill them, that no memorie,
No black and blasted infamy hereafter—

ARCHAS
Come, are ye ready?

BOROSKIE
Yes.

ARCHAS
And truly penitent, to make your way straight?

BOROSKIE
Thus I wash off my sins.

ARCHAS
Stand up, and live then,
And live an honest man; I scorn mens ruines:
Take him again, Sir, trie him: and believe
This thing will be a perfect man.

DUKE
I take him.

BOROSKIE
And when I fail those hopes, heavens hopes fail me.

DUKE
You are old: no more wars Father:
Theodore take you the charge, be General.

THEODORE
All good bless ye.

DUKE
And my good Father, you dwell in my bosom,
From you rise all my good thoughts: when I would think
And examine time for one that's fairly noble,
And the same man through all the streights of vertue,
Upon this Silver book I'le look, and read him.
Now forward merrily to Hymens rites,
To joyes, and revels, sports, and he that can
Most honour Archas, is the noblest man.

[Exeunt.

EPILOGUE

Though something well assur'd, few here repent

Three hours of pretious time, or money spent
On our endeavours, Yet not to relye
Too much upon our care, and industrie,
'Tis fit we should ask, but a modest way
How you approve our action in the play.
If you vouchsafe to crown it with applause,
It is your bountie, and you give us cause
Hereafter with a general consent
To study, as becomes us, your content.

John Fletcher – A Short Biography

John Fletcher was born in December, 1579 in Rye, Sussex. He was baptised on December 20th.

As can be imagined details of much of his life and career have not survived and, accordingly, only a very brief indication of his life and works can be given.

His father, Richard Fletcher, was a successful and rather ambitious cleric. From being the Dean of Peterborough he moved on to become the Bishop of Bristol, Bishop of Worcester and finally, shortly before his death, the Bishop of London. He was also the chaplain to Queen Elizabeth.

When he was Dean of Peterborough, Richard Fletcher, witnessed the execution of Mary, Queen of Scots. It was said he "knelt down on the scaffold steps and started to pray out loud and at length, in a prolonged and rhetorical style, as though determined to force his way into the pages of history". He cried out at her death, "So perish all the Queen's enemies!" All very dramatic but the family did have strong links to the Arts.

Young Fletcher appears at the very young age of eleven to have entered Corpus Christi College at Cambridge University in 1591. There are no records that he ever took a degree but there is some small evidence that he was being prepared for a career in the church.

However what is clear is that this was soon abandoned as he joined the stream of people who would leave University and decamp to the more bohemian life of commercial theatre in London.

Unfortunately his father fell out with Queen Elizabeth but appears to have been on his way to rehabilitation before his death in 1596. At his death he was, however, mired in debt.

The upbringing of the now teenage Fletcher and his seven siblings now passed to his paternal uncle, the poet and minor official Giles Fletcher. Giles, who had the patronage of the Earl of Essex may have been a liability rather than an advantage to the young Fletcher. With Essex involved in the failed rebellion against Elizabeth Giles was also tainted by association.

By 1606 John Fletcher appears to have equipped himself with the talents to become a playwright. Initially this appears to have been for the Children of the Queen's Revels, then performing at the Blackfriars Theatre.

Commendatory verses by Richard Brome in the Beaumont and Fletcher 1647 folio place Fletcher in the company of Ben Jonson, although it is not known when this friendship began. Jonson, of course, was a leviathan of English Literature, so admired that many of his literary friends and colleagues were simply known as 'Sons of Ben'. Fletcher's frequent early collaborator, Francis Beaumont, was also a friend of Jonson's.

Fletcher's early career was marked by one significant failure; The Faithful Shepherdess, his adaptation of Giovanni Battista Guarini's Il Pastor Fido, which was performed by the Blackfriars Children in 1608. In the preface to the printed edition of his play, Fletcher explained the failure as due to his audience's faulty expectations. They expected a pastoral tragicomedy to feature dances, comedy, and murder, with the shepherds presented in conventional stereotypes – as Fletcher put it, wearing "gray cloaks, with curtailed dogs in strings." Fletcher's preface is however best known for its pithy definition of tragicomedy: "A tragicomedy is not so called in respect of mirth and killing, but in respect it wants [i.e., lacks] deaths, which is enough to make it no tragedy; yet brings some near it, which is enough to make it no comedy." A comedy, he went on to say, must be "a representation of familiar people." His preface is critical of drama that features characters whose action violates nature.

In that case, Fletcher appears to have been developing a new style faster than audiences could comprehend. By 1609, however, he had found his stride. With Beaumont, he wrote Philaster, which became a hit for the King's Men and began a profitable association between Fletcher and that company. Philaster appears also to have begun a trend for tragicomedy. Fletcher's influence has also been said to have inspired some features of Shakespeare's late romances, and certainly his influence on the tragicomic work of other playwrights is even more marked.

By the middle of the 1610s, Fletcher's plays had achieved a popularity that rivalled Shakespeare's and cemented the pre-eminence of the King's Men in Jacobean London. After Beaumont's retirement, necessitated by ill-health, and then his early death in 1616, Fletcher continued working, both singly and in collaboration, until his death in 1625. By that time, he had produced, or had been credited with, close to fifty plays. This body of work remained a major part of the King's Men's repertory until the closing of the theatres in 1642 due to the Civil War.

At the beginning of his career Fletcher's most important collaborator was Francis Beaumont. The two wrote together for close to a decade, first for the Children of the Queen's Revels, and then for the King's Men. According to an anecdote transmitted or invented by John Aubrey, they also lived together in Bankside, sharing clothes and having "one wench in the house between them." This domestic arrangement, if it existed, was ended by Beaumont's marriage in 1613, and their dramatic partnership ended after Beaumont fell ill, probably of a stroke, that same year.

At this point Fletcher had written many plays with Beaumont and several others on his own. He seems to have been regarded as quite a talent although it should be remembered that playwrights were required to be prolific, to easily work with other collaborators and to produce work of quality and commercial appeal very quickly.

The King's Men, run by Philip Henslowe, was the most prestigious of the theatre companies and Fletcher now had an increasingly close association with it.

Fletcher collaborated with Shakespeare on Henry VIII, The Two Noble Kinsmen, and the now lost Cardenio, which some scholars say was the basis for Lewis Theobald's play Double Falsehood. (Theobald is regarded as one of the best Shakespearean editors. Whether his play is based on Cardenio or on some other is not absolutely known although Theobald certainly promoted it as his revision of the lost Shakespeare/Fletcher play.)

A play that Fletcher also wrote by himself at this time, The Woman's Prize or the Tamer Tamed, is also regarded as a sequel to The Taming of the Shrew.

In 1616, with the death of Shakespeare, Fletcher now appears to have entered into an enhanced arrangement with the King's Men on very similar terms to Shakespeare's. Fletcher would now write exclusively for the King's Men until his own death almost a decade later.

As well as continuing his solo productions Fletcher was still collaborating with other playwrights, mainly Philip Massinger, who, in turn, would succeed him as the in-house playwright for the King's Men.

Fletcher's popularity continued throughout his life; indeed during the winter of 1621, he had three of his plays performed at court. His mastery is most notable in two dramatic types; tragicomedy and the comedy of manners.

John Fletcher died in 1625, it is thought of bubonic plague which, at the time, was undergoing further outbreaks.

He seems to have been buried in what is now Southwark Cathedral, although a precise location is not known. There is much made of an anecdote that Fletcher and Massinger (who died in 1640) share the same grave but it is more likely that both are buried within a few yards of each other and that the stone markers in the floor have confused the issue. One is marked 'Edmond Shakespeare 1607' and the other 'John Fletcher 1625' refers to Shakespeare's younger brother and the playwright. The churchyards were, more often than not, completely over-crowded and breeding grounds for disease. Precise record keeping was not a practiced skill.

During the later Commonwealth, many of the playwright's best-known scenes were kept alive as drolls. These were brief performances, usually condensed into one or two scenes and with the addition of music or song to satisfy the taste for plays while the theatres were closed under the Puritans. At the re-opening of the theatres in 1660, the plays in the Fletcher canon, in original form or revised, were by far the most common productions on the English stage. The most frequently revived plays suggest the developing taste for comedies of manners. Among the tragedies, The Maid's Tragedy and, especially, Rollo Duke of Normandy held the stage. Four tragicomedies (A King and No King, The Humorous Lieutenant, Philaster, and The Island Princess) were popular, perhaps in part for their similarity to and foreshadowing of heroic drama. Four comedies (Rule a Wife And Have a Wife, The Chances, Beggars' Bush, and especially The Scornful Lady) were also stage mainstays.

Despite his popularity, and it appears he was held in higher regard than Shakespeare at this time, his works steadily lost ground to those of Shakespeare and to new productions from other playwrights.

Since then Fletcher has increasingly become a subject only for occasional revivals and for specialists. Fletcher and his collaborators have been the subject of important bibliographic and critical studies, but the plays have been revived only infrequently.

Due to the frequent collaborations between all manner of playwrights, and the revisions carried out in later years, having a settled list of authorship to any given set of plays can be problematic. The works of Fletcher and others of this period most definitely fall into this category. It is as well to take into account that during this period theatres were quite often closed either due to outbreaks of the plague or to the prevailing political and moral climate. Printers, anxious to provide materials that would sell, were not above changing a name or two to enhance sales.

Although Fletcher collaborated most often with Beaumont and Massinger, it is believed that Massinger revised many of the plays some time after their original production. Other collaborators including Nathan Field, William Shakespeare, William Rowley and others also can be seen distinctly in Fletchers' works. Many modern scholars point out that Fletcher had many particular mannerisms but other playwrights would also duplicate these at times so allocating exact contributions of anyone to a play is somewhat of a detective case in many instances. However from the original folio printings or licensing via the Master of the Revels (the statutory licensing authority to approve and censor plays as well a hand in publication and printing of theatrical materials) as well as contemporary notes a fairly precise bibliography of the works can be given with only a few plays lacking substantial authority and provenance.

John Fletcher – A Concise Bibliography

This bibliography gives the most likely date of writing together with when published, revised or licensed by the Master or the Revels (This position within the royal household was originally for royal festivities, ie revels, and later to oversee stage censorship, until this function was transferred to the Lord Chamberlain in 1624).

Solo Plays

The Faithful Shepherdess, pastoral (written 1608–9; printed 1609)
The Tragedy of Valentinian, tragedy (1610–14; 1647)
Monsieur Thomas, comedy (c. 1610–16; 1639)
The Woman's Prize, or The Tamer Tamed, comedy (c. 1611; 1647)
Bonduca, tragedy (1611–14; 1647)
The Chances, comedy (c. 1613–25; 1647)
Wit Without Money, comedy (c. 1614; 1639)
The Mad Lover, tragicomedy (acted 5 January 1617; 1647)
The Loyal Subject, tragicomedy (licensed 16 November 1618; revised 1633; 1647)
The Humorous Lieutenant, tragicomedy (c. 1619; 1647)
Women Pleased, tragicomedy (c. 1619–23; 1647)
The Island Princess, tragicomedy (c. 1620; 1647)
The Wild Goose Chase, comedy (c. 1621; 1652)
The Pilgrim, comedy (c. 1621; 1647)
A Wife for a Month, tragicomedy (licensed 27 May 1624; 1647)
Rule a Wife and Have a Wife, comedy (licensed 19 October 1624; 1640)

Collaborations

With Francis Beaumont
The Woman Hater, comedy (1606; 1607)
Cupid's Revenge, tragedy (c. 1607–12; 1615)
Philaster, or Love Lies a-Bleeding, tragicomedy (c. 1609; 1620)
The Maid's Tragedy, Tragedy (c. 1609; 1619)
A King and No King, tragicomedy (1611; 1619)
The Captain, comedy (c. 1609–12; 1647)
The Scornful Lady, comedy (c. 1613; 1616)
Love's Pilgrimage, tragicomedy (c. 1615–16; 1647)
The Noble Gentleman, comedy (c. 1613; licensed 3 February 1626; 1647)

With Francis Beaumont & Philip Massinger
Thierry & Theodoret, tragedy (c. 1607; 1621)
The Coxcomb, comedy (c. 1608–10; 1647)
Beggars' Bush, comedy (c. 1612–13; revised 1622; 1647)
Love's Cure, comedy (c. 1612–13; revised 1625; 1647)

With Philip Massinger
Sir John van Olden Barnavelt, tragedy (August 1619; MS)
The Little French Lawyer, comedy (c. 1619–23; 1647)
A Very Woman, tragicomedy (c. 1619–22; licensed 6 June 1634; 1655)
The Custom of the Country, comedy (c. 1619–23; 1647)
The Double Marriage, tragedy (c. 1619–23; 1647)
The False One, history (c. 1619–23; 1647)
The Prophetess, tragicomedy (licensed 14 May 1622; 1647)
The Sea Voyage, comedy (licensed 22 June 1622; 1647)
The Spanish Curate, comedy (licensed 24 October 1622; 1647)
The Lovers' Progress or The Wandering Lovers, tragicomedy (licensed 6 December 1623; rev 1634; 1647)
The Elder Brother, comedy (c. 1625; 1637)

With Philip Massinger & Nathan Field
The Honest Man's Fortune, tragicomedy (1613; 1647)
The Queen of Corinth, tragicomedy (c. 1616–18; 1647)
The Knight of Malta, tragicomedy (c. 1619; 1647)

With William Shakespeare
Henry VIII, history (c. 1613; 1623)
The Two Noble Kinsmen, tragicomedy (c. 1613; 1634)
Cardenio, tragicomedy (c. 1613)

With Thomas Middleton & William Rowley
Wit at Several Weapons, comedy (c. 1610–20; 1647)

With William Rowley
The Maid in the Mill (licensed 29 August 1623; 1647).

With Nathan Field
Four Plays, or Moral Representations, in One, morality (c. 1608–13; 1647)

With Philip Massinger, Ben Jonson and George Chapman
Rollo Duke of Normandy, or The Bloody Brother, tragedy (c. 1617; revised 1627–30; 1639)

With James Shirley
The Night Walker, or The Little Thief, comedy (c. 1611; 1640)
The Coronation c. 1635

Uncertain
The Nice Valour, or The Passionate Madman, comedy (c. 1615–25; 1647)
The Laws of Candy, tragicomedy (c. 1619–23; 1647)
The Fair Maid of the Inn, comedy (licensed 22 January 1626; 1647)
The Faithful Friends, tragicomedy (registered 29 June 1660; MS.)

The Nice Valour is possibly by Fletcher revised by Thomas Middleton;

The Fair Maid of the Inn is perhaps a play by Massinger, John Ford, and John Webster, either with or without Fletcher's involvement.

The Laws of Candy has been variously attributed to Fletcher and to John Ford.

The Night-Walker was a Fletcher original, with additions by Shirley for a 1639 production.

Even now there is not absolute certainty on several of the plays. The first Beaumont & Fletcher folio of 1647 contained 35 plays and the second folio of 1679 added a further 18. In total 53 plays.

The first folio included The Masque of the Inner Temple and Gray's Inn (1613), and the second The Knight of the Burning Pestle (1607), widely considered Beaumont's solo works, although the latter was in early editions attributed to both writers. Fletcher himself said that Beaumont was attributed so-authorship of many works that belonged solely to Fletcher or to other collaborators.

One play in the canon, Sir John Van Olden Barnavelt, existed in manuscript and was not published till 1883.